WHO MADE GOD?

Also by Ravi Zacharias and Norman Geisler

Is Your Church Ready? Motivating Leaders to Live an Apologetic Life

WHO MADE GOD?

AND ANSWERS
TO OVER
100
OTHER TOUGH
QUESTIONS
OF FAITH

RAVI ZACHARIAS
NORMAN GEISLER
GENERAL EDITORS

ZONDERVAN™

GRAND RAPIDS, MICHIGAN 49530 USA

We want to hear from you. Please send your comments about this book to us in care of zreview@zondervan.com. Thank you.

ZONDERVAN™

Who Made God?
Copyright © 2003 by Ravi Zacharias and Norman Geisler

Requests for information should be addressed to:
Zondervan, *Grand Rapids, Michigan 49530*

Library of Congress Cataloging-in-Publication Data

Who made God? : and answers to over 100 other tough questions of faith / Ravi Zacharias and Norman Geisler, general editors.—1st ed.
    p. cm.
Includes bibliographical references and index.
ISBN 0-310-24710-1
    1. Apologetics. 2. Christianity—Miscellanea. I. Zacharias, Ravi K. II. Geisler, Norman L.
BT1103.W48 2003
239—dc21

                          2003008436

Published in association with the literary agency of Wolgemuth & Associates, Inc.

Interior design by Tracey Moran

Printed in the United States of America

---

04 05 06 07 08 09 /❖ DC/ 10 9 8

CONTENTS

Part 2: Questions about Other Faiths

PREFACE

I all too clearly remember the day when, as a lad growing up in India, my mother had put a delicious treat into my hand. Happily, I walked outside, enjoying every juicy bite and wishing it would never come to an end. Suddenly, out of nowhere, an eagle swooped down upon me, and faster than the eye could see or the mind could react, the food was gone from my hand and the side of my face was clawed. I stood there completely shaken by the experience. My instinctive reaction was to run home, crying and calling for my mother's comfort and hoping for help and replenishment. What I got was a stiff warning to always be mindful of such ever-circling predators that could in a moment leave you empty-handed.

This experience came to mind as I thought of the losses our culture has suffered over the last three decades. As Christians we happily wandered throughout the land with the Bible in our hands, preaching it yet leaving it unprotected from the vandals who sought to snatch it and leave us somewhat disoriented. For many in our midst, that is a true portrayal of the scenario, and they stagger into our churches looking for rescue and solace.

Paul exhorted Timothy to guard the trust that he had been given (see 1 Timothy 6:20). We, no less, are called upon to do the same in these times. Therefore, when Norman Geisler first suggested that we be coeditors of this book, I reacted with both delight and fear—delight because the book was needed, and fear because Norman Geisler was my professor during my days at graduate school. He has since been a teacher, both in his writings and as a resource for anything I have needed in my study of Christian apologetics. My culture has influenced me to believe that a student appears rather audacious to have his name alongside one from whom he has learned. One can never repay the debt to his instructor. I agreed to be part of this project with much trepidation but with the deepest gratitude for what I have learned from him and others.

I say all this to underscore that we live in a time when the church desperately needs to be taught in this field, and in a study such as this one we have access to some of the finest minds. To state the obvious, we could have added a number of other contributors. But we have drawn from a limited number to keep the size manageable, and we have, I believe, a wonderful reservoir here presented by thinkers who are also practitioners.

To learn from these men is a privilege. They help us guard the trust of the glorious gospel of Jesus Christ. If we do not learn how to guard it, we will be shedding tears and bemoaning the fact that the claws of skepticism have snatched from our hands the nourishing Word that is the only hope by which society can survive. I pay tribute to Dr. Geisler and to the others who have given us their insight on themes as important as these. It is an honor to be part of this venture. May their collective efforts make us all better equipped to bring the beauty and the power of the gospel to a confused and troubled world.

Ravi K. Zacharias

Acknowledgments

Many have contributed to this effort. In the early days, Joan Cattell, research assistant to Norman Geisler, labored hard to get every contributor's work in place. Her patience was a good example of an apologist with a kindly disposition. Danielle DuRant, Ravi Zacharias's research assistant, served as managing editor and worked unselfishly and around the clock to get the manuscript to the publisher in a well-organized and completed form. Without her, we never would have met all the deadlines. Our sincere thanks go out to her. The contributors to this volume and Zondervan's editorial staff deserve our heartfelt thanks as well. We are grateful to God that the work finally hit the press.

NOTE: Not all views expressed in these chapters reflect the views shared by the editors.

Contributors

William Lane Craig

William Lane Craig is a research professor of philosophy at Talbot School of Theology in La Mirada, California. He earned a doctorate in philosophy at the University of Birmingham, England, before taking a doctorate in theology from the Ludwig-Maximilians-Universität in München, Germany, at which he was for two years a fellow of the Alexander von Humboldt-Stiftung. Prior to his appointment at Talbot, he spent seven years at the Higher Institute of Philosophy of the Katholieke Universiteit in Leuven, Belgium. He has authored more than a dozen books, including *The Kalam Cosmological Argument; Divine Foreknowledge and Human Freedom;* and *Theism, Atheism, and Big Bang Cosmology,* as well as nearly a hundred articles in professional journals of philosophy and theology, including *The Journal of Philosophy, American Philosophical Quarterly, Philosophical Studies, Philosophy,* and *British Journal for Philosophy of Science.*

Norman Geisler

Norman Geisler is an award-winning author and coauthor of over fifty books and hundreds of articles. He has taught at the university and graduate level for forty-three years and has spoken or debated in all fifty states and in twenty-six countries. Educated at William Tyndale College and Wheaton Graduate School, he holds a Ph.D. in philosophy from Loyola University and now serves as president of Southern Evangelical Seminary in Charlotte, North Carolina. Many of Dr. Geisler's works are used as textbooks in Christian colleges and seminaries, including such books as *A General Introduction* to the Bible, When Skeptics Ask, When Critics Ask, Christian Apologetics, and Baker Encyclopedia of Christian Apologetics.

Lawrence Theodore Jeyachandran

L. T. Jeyachandran is the missions director for Ravi Zacharias International Ministries in Singapore. He hails from South India and received a master of technology degree in structural engineering from the Indian Institute of Technology, a premier engineering school in Chennai. Jeyachandran worked in several parts of India for twenty-eight years as a senior civil engineer with the central (federal) government. He took early retirement from the government in 1993 to join RZIM in India as director of ministries. He is a keen student of theology and comparative religions and is also interested in the study of the Indian language as well as other foreign languages.

Ronald Rhodes

Dr. Ronald Rhodes is president of Reasoning from the Scriptures Ministries, an apologetics organization located in Frisco, Texas. He has taught courses at such institutions as Biola University, Southern Evangelical Seminary, and Dallas Theological Seminary. His books include The Complete Book of Bible Answers, The Challenge of the Cults and New Religions, Reasoning from the Scriptures with Jehovah's Witnesses, and Find It Fast: Handy Bible Encyclopedia.

Lee Strobel

Lee Strobel is an award-winning author, sought-after speaker, and teaching pastor at Saddleback Valley Community Church in Orange County, California, where he regularly speaks to the fifteen thousand seekers and Christians who visit each weekend. A former atheist, he holds a master of studies in law degree from Yale Law School, and he was the award-winning legal editor of the *Chicago Tribune* before his conversion in 1981. His books include two Gold Medallion winners: *Inside the Mind of Unchurched Harry & Mary* and *The Case for Christ,* which rose to number one on the Christian books best-seller list. Strobel's other books include *God's Outrageous Claim, What Jesus Would Say,* and *The Case for Faith.* He is a founding board member of the Willow Creek Association, a network of five thousand churches striving to communicate Christianity to spiritual seekers, and the host of *Defining Moments,* a monthly audio journal for church leaders.

Robert White

Robert White graduated from Auburn University in Montgomery, Alabama, with a B.S. in criminal justice, and from Jones School of Law (also in Montgomery) with a juris doctorate. While at Jones he was voted president of the Christian Legal Society and student representative for the Alabama Lawyers Association. He was called into the ministry in 1994 and is an ordained minister under the auspices of the Southern Baptist Convention. He developed and produced a youth-oriented radio talk show called *Saved by Grace* and has assisted several local ministries in conducting evangelism and community development projects. Robert White is currently a pastor's assistant at Central Community Christian Church in Montgomery.

Part 1

Questions about the Christian Faith

Chapter 1

TOUGH QUESTIONS ABOUT GOD

NORMAN GEISLER

My daughter Ruth, a pastor's wife, told her oldest son, Samuel, who was then about four years old, "Go ask your grandfather." A moment later I was confronted with this tough question: "Grandpa, where is the mind in the brain?" This question is easy enough to answer for a college or seminary philosophy student who knows what a category mistake is, but how do you explain it to a four-year-old?

As parents and church leaders who have ministered to small children know, the toughest questions typically come from the youngest members of the congregation. Often these are about God—such as, "Daddy, who made God?" More than a few parents have heard this question before, but only a few can answer it.

We must be prepared to give an answer (1 Peter 3:15) to every sincere question we are asked (Colossians 4:6). Here are some of the toughest ones I've been asked over the past fifty years of ministry. I will try my best to answer them so that even young boys and girls can understand.

WHO MADE GOD?

Who made God? No one did. He was not made. He has always existed. Only things that had a beginning—like the world—need a maker. God had no beginning, so God did not need to be made.

For those who are a little older, a little more can be said. Traditionally, most atheists who deny the existence of God believe that the universe was not made; it was just "there" forever. They appeal to the first law of thermodynamics for support: "Energy can neither be created nor destroyed," they insist. Several things must be observed in response.

First, this way of stating the first law is not scientific; rather, it is a philosophical assertion. Science is based on observation, and there is no observational evidence that can support the dogmatic "can" and "cannot" implicit in this statement. It should read, "[As far as we have observed,] the amount of actual energy in the universe remains constant." That is, no one had observed any actual new energy either coming into existence or going out of existence. Once the first law is understood properly, it says nothing about the universe being eternal or having no beginning. As far as the first law is concerned, energy may or may not have been created. It simply asserts that if energy was created, then as far as we can tell, the actual amount of energy that was created has remained constant since then.

Further, let us suppose for the sake of argument that energy—the whole universe of energy we call the cosmos—was not created, as many atheists have traditionally believed. If this is so, it is meaningless to ask who made the universe. If energy is eternal and uncreated, of course no one created it. It has always existed. However, if it is meaningless to ask, "Who made the universe?" since it has always existed, then it is equally meaningless to ask "Who made God?" since he has always existed.

If the universe is not eternal, it needs a cause. On the other hand, if it has no beginning, it does not need a cause of its beginning. Likewise, if a God exists who has no beginning, it is absurd to ask, "Who made God?" It is a category mistake to ask, "Who made the Unmade?" or "Who created the Uncreated?" One may as well ask, "Where is the bachelor's wife?"

WHY COULDN'T THE WORLD ALWAYS HAVE EXISTED?

Christians naturally believe there must be a God because the world had a beginning. And everything that had a beginning had a beginner. But the tough question to answer is how we know the world had a beginning. Maybe the world always existed.

Famous agnostic Bertrand Russell presented this dilemma: Either the world had a beginning, or it did not. If it did not, it did not need a cause (God). If it did, we can ask, "Who caused God?" But if God has a cause, he is not God. In either case, we do not arrive at a first uncaused cause (God).

The answer to this tough question is that it, too, asks a meaningless question: Who made God? To put it another way, it wrongly assumes that *"everything* must have a cause" when what is claimed is that *"everything that had a beginning* had a cause." This is quite a different matter. Of course, everything that had a beginning had a beginner. Nothing cannot make something. As Julie Andrews once sang, "Nothing came from nothing. Nothing ever could." So God does not need a cause because he had no beginning.

This being the case, we need only to show that the universe had a beginning, to show that there must have been a cause of it (i.e., God). Two strong arguments will be offered as evidence that the universe had a beginning. One is from science—the second law of thermodynamics. The second is from philosophy, namely, the impossibility of an infinite number of moments.

According to the second law of thermodynamics, the universe is running out of usable energy.[1] But if the universe is running down, it cannot be eternal. Otherwise, it would have run down completely by now. While you can never run out of an unlimited amount of energy, it does not take forever to run out of a limited amount of energy. Hence, the universe must have had a beginning. To illustrate, every car has a limited amount of energy (gas). That is why we have to refuel from time to time—more often than we like. If we had an unlimited (i.e., infinitely) large gas tank, we would never have to stop for gas again. The fact that we have to refill shows that it was filled up to begin with. Or, to use another example, an old clock that gradually unwinds and has to be rewound would not unwind unless it had been wound up to begin with. In short, the universe had a beginning. And whatever had a beginning must have had a beginner. Therefore, the universe must have had a beginner (God).

Some have speculated that the universe is self-winding or self-rebounding. But this position is exactly that—pure speculation without any real evidence. In fact, it is contrary to the second law of thermodynamics. For even if the universe were rebounding, like a bouncing ball in reverse, it would gradually peter out. There is simply no observational evidence that the universe is self-winding. Even agnostic astronomers like Robert Jastrow have pointed out: "Once hydrogen has been burned within that star and converted to heavier elements, it can never be restored to its original state." Thus, "minute by minute and year by year, as hydrogen is used up in stars, the supply of this element grows smaller."[2]

If the overall amount of actual energy stays the same but the universe is running out of usable energy, it has never had an infinite amount—for an infinite amount of energy can never run down. This would mean that the universe could not have existed forever in the past. It must have had a beginning. Or, to put it another way, according to the second law, since the universe is getting more and more disordered, it cannot be eternal. Otherwise, it would be totally disordered by now, which it is not. So it must have had a beginning—one that was highly ordered.

A second argument that the universe had a beginning—and hence a beginner—comes from philosophy. It argues that there could not have been an infinite number of moments before today; otherwise today never would have come (which it has). This is because, by definition, an infinite can never be traversed—it has no end (or beginning). But since the moments before today have been traversed—that is, we have arrived at today—it follows that there must only have been a finite (limited) number of moments before today. That is, time had a beginning. But if the space-time universe had a beginning, it must have been caused to come into existence. This cause of everything else that exists is called God. God exists.

Even the great skeptic David Hume held both premises of this argument for God. What is more, Hume himself never denied that things have a cause for their existence. He wrote, "I never asserted so absurd a proposition as that anything might arise without a cause."[3] He also said that it was absurd to believe there were an infinite number of moments: "The temporal world has a beginning. An infinite number of real parts of time, passing in succession and exhausted one after another, appears so evident a contradiction that no man, one should think, whose judgment is not corrupted, instead of being improved, by the sciences, would ever be able to admit it."[4] Now if both of these premises are true, it follows that there must have been a creator of the space-time universe we call the cosmos—that is, God exists.

HOW CAN GOD MAKE SOMETHING OUT OF NOTHING?

If God and nothing else existed prior to the creation of the world, the universe came into existence from nothing. But isn't it absurd to say that something can come from nothing? It is absurd to say that nothing caused something, because nothing does not exist and has no power to do anything. But it is not absurd to say that someone (i.e., God) brought the universe into existence from nonexistence. Nothing cannot make something, but someone (i.e., God) can make something out of nothing.

In fact, if the universe had a beginning (as demonstrated earlier), then there was once no universe and then there was—after God created it. This is what is meant by creation "out of nothing" (Latin, *ex nihilo*). It does not mean that God took a "handful of nothing" and made something out of it, as though "nothing" were something out of which he made the world. There was God and simply nothing else. Then God brought something else into existence that had not existed to that point.

Or to put it another way, creation "out of nothing" simply means that God did not create out of something else that which already existed alongside himself, as in certain forms of dualism in which there are two eternal substances of entities. This is really creation *ex materia,* that is, out of some preexisting matter outside of God. The Greek philosopher Plato held this view.

Neither did God create the world out of himself (i.e., *ex Deo*). That is, God did not take part of himself and make the world out of it. In fact, the orthodox Christian God has no parts. He is a simple whole that is absolutely one. Thus there is no way God could have taken part of himself and made the world. God is infinite and the world is finite. And no amount of finite parts can make an infinite, since no matter how many parts or pieces one has, there could always be one more. But there cannot be more than an infinite. Hence, no amount of parts would ever equal an infinite. So God could not have created the world out of part of himself (i.e., *ex materia*).

The world came *from* God but is not *of* God. He was its cause but not its substance. It came into existence *by* him, but it is not made *of* him. However, if the world was not created out of God *(ex Deo)* or out of something else *(ex materia)* existing alongside God, it must have been created out of nothing *(ex nihilo)*. There is no other alternative. God made something that before he made it did not exist, either in him or in anything else.

The only place the world "existed" before God made it was as an idea in God's mind. Just as a painter has an idea of his painting in his mind before he paints it, so God had an idea of the world before he made it. In this sense, the world preexisted in God's mind as an idea before he brought it into existence.

WHAT WAS GOD DOING BEFORE HE MADE THE WORLD?

Another tough question often asked about God is this: What was God doing with all his time before he created? The famous fifth-century A.D. Christian teacher Augustine had two answers to this question, one humorous and one serious. The first answer was that God was spending his time preparing hell for people who ask questions like this! The serious answer was that God didn't have any time on his hands, since there was no time before time was created. Time began with creation. Before creation, time did not exist. So there was no time for God to have on his hands. The world did not begin by a creation *in* time but by a creation *of* time. *But,* you may think, *if there was no time before time began, what was there?* The answer is, eternity. God is eternal, and the only thing prior to time was eternity.

Further, the question implies that an infinitely perfect being like God could get bored. Boredom, however, is a sign of imperfection and dissatisfaction, and God is perfectly satisfied. Thus, there is no way God could be bored, even if he had long time periods on his hands. An infinitely creative mind can always find something interesting to do. Only finite minds that run out of interesting things to do get bored.

Finally, the Christian God has three persons who are in perfect fellowship. There is no way such a being could get bored or lonely. There is not only always someone to "talk to," but someone of perfect understanding, love, and companionship. Boredom is impossible in such a being.

HOW CAN THERE BE THREE PERSONS IN ONE GOD?

How can God be three and yet one? Isn't this a contradiction? It would seem that God could be one and not three, or three and not one. But he cannot be both three and one at the same time. It would be a violation of the most fundamental law of thought, namely, the law of noncontradiction.

First of all, the Christian belief in a Trinity of three persons in one God is not a contradiction. A contradiction occurs only when something is both A and non-A at the same time and in the same sense. God is both three and one at the same time but not *in the same sense.* He is three persons but one in essence. He is three persons but only one in nature.

It would be a contradiction to say that God had three natures in one nature or three persons in one person. But it is not a contradiction to claim that God has three persons in one nature. God is like a triangle. At the same time it has three corners and yet it is only one triangle. Each corner is not the same as the whole triangle. Or, God is like one to the third power (1^3). $1 \times 1 \times 1 = 1$. God is not $1 + 1 + 1 = 3$, which is tritheism or polytheism. God is one God, manifested eternally and simultaneously in three distinct persons.

God is love (1 John 4:16). But to have love, there must be a lover (Father), a loved one (Son), and a spirit of love (Holy Spirit). So, love itself is a tri-unity.

Another illustration of the Trinity is that God is like my mind, ideas, and words. There is a unity between them, yet they are distinct from each other.

Of course, the Trinity is a mystery. It goes beyond reason without going against reason. We can apprehend it, but we cannot completely comprehend it. As someone wisely said, "If we try to understand God completely, we may lose our mind, but if we do not believe in the Trinity sincerely, we will lose our soul!"

HOW CAN A GOOD GOD SEND PEOPLE TO HELL?

This question assumes that God sends people to hell against their will. But this is not the case. God desires everyone to be saved (see 2 Peter 3:9). Those who are not saved do not will to be saved. Jesus said, "O Jerusalem, Jerusalem, you who kill the prophets and stone those sent to you, how often I have longed to gather your children together, as a hen gathers her chicks under her wings, but you were not willing" (Matthew 23:37).

As C. S. Lewis put it, "The door of hell is locked on the inside." All who go there choose to do so. Lewis added: "There are only two kinds of people in the end: those who say to God, 'Thy will be done,' and those to whom God says, in the end, '*Thy* will be done.' All that are in hell, choose it." Lewis believed "without that self-choice there could be no hell. No soul that seriously and constantly desires joy will ever miss it. Those who seek find. To those who knock it is opened."[5]

Furthermore, heaven would be hell for those who are not fitted for it. For heaven is a place of constant praise and worship of God (Revelation 4–5). But for unbelievers who do not enjoy one hour of worship a week on earth, it would be hell to force them to do this forever in heaven! Hear Lewis again: "I would pay any price to be able to say truthfully 'All will be saved.' But my reason retorts, 'Without their will, or with it?' If I say 'Without their will,' I at once perceive a contradiction; how can the supreme voluntary act of self-surrender be involuntary? If I say 'With their will,' my reason replies 'How if they *will not* give in?'"[6]

God is just and he must punish sin (Habakkuk 1:13; Revelation 20:11–15). But he is also love (1 John 4:16), and his love cannot force others to love him. Love cannot work coercively but only persuasively. Forced love is a contradiction in terms. Hence, God's love demands that there be a hell where persons who do not wish to love him can experience the great divorce when God says to them, "Thy will be done!"

HOW CAN GOD BE BOTH LOVING AND JUST?

It would seem that love and justice are incompatible attributes. If God is just, he must punish sin. But if he is loving, he would forgive sin. How then can he be both?

The attributes (characteristics) of God are not contradictory. He is both absolutely just and yet unconditionally loving. Each attribute complements the other. God is "justly holy" and "holy just." That is, his justice is administered in love, and his love is distributed justly.

The perfect example of how God's love and justice kiss is in the cross. In his love, God sent his Son to pay the penalty for our sins so that his justice could be satisfied and his love released. For "the wages of sin is death" (Romans 6:23). And sin against the eternal God demands eternal death (see Revelation 20:14–15). So when Christ died for our sins (see Romans 5:8), the Just suffered for the unjust (see 1 Peter 3:18) that he might bring us to God. "God made him who had no sin to be sin for us, so that in him we might become the righteousness of God" (2 Corinthians 5:21).

God's justice demands that sin be punished, but his love compels him to save sinners. So by Christ's death for us his justice is satisfied and his love released. Thus, there is no contradiction between absolute justice and unconditional love. To illustrate, God is like the judge who, after passing out the punishment to the guilty defendant, laid aside his robe, stood alongside the convicted, and paid the fine for him. Jesus did the same for us on Calvary. Surely justice and mercy kissed at the cross.

Conclusion

Even little children like my grandson can ask tough questions, but there are good answers for all these "God questions." And the Bible exhorts us to find them and give them. Paul wrote, "Let your conversation be always full of grace, seasoned with salt, so that you may know how to answer everyone" (Colossians 4:6).

By the way, my grandson just graduated from college and is preparing to attend seminary to study apologetics (defending the faith). Soon he will be prepared to answer the same kinds of questions he asked. One can only wonder what he would be doing if no one had answered his.

QUESTIONS FOR REFLECTION AND DISCUSSION

1. Read 1 Peter 3:15 and Colossians 4:6. Given that these verses are addressed to all believers, what can we do to put them into practice?
2. When, if ever, should questions asked by unbelievers not be answered? Consider Proverbs 26:4 and Matthew 7:6 in your response.
3. Why is it so important to answer questions about God? How does belief in God relate to our belief that the Bible is the Word of God and that Jesus Christ is the Son of God?

Chapter 2

TOUGH QUESTIONS ABOUT EVIL

RONALD RHODES

In early 1999 my brother's son Greg was hit by a car and killed. After the funeral service, the question that lingered on the minds of mourning family members and friends was "Why did something like this have to happen?" It is the same question people through the ages have asked whenever tragedy strikes: Why do bad things happen to good people? And what does it say about God that such things occur? Just think what the friends and relatives of the almost three thousand people who lost their lives in the terrorist attacks in New York and Washington on September 11, 2001, must have wrestled with. Pollster George Barna was once commissioned to inquire of people what one question they would ask of God if they had the opportunity. By an overwhelming margin, the most urgent question was: "Why is there so much suffering in the world?"[1]

My goal is to briefly examine some of the tough questions about evil. I approach this subject with some hesitation in view of the fact that a proper treatment requires a full book, not just a short chapter. Abbreviated treatments always run the risk of superficiality. I urge the reader to supplement my brief treatment with some of the more exhaustive works cited in the endnotes and in the suggested resources listed at the back of this book.

Before getting to the questions, it may be good to record a few preliminary thoughts about evil. Evil is not something that has an existence all its own; rather, it is a corruption of that which already exists. *Evil is the absence or privation of something good.* Rot, for example, can exist only as long as the tree exists. Tooth decay can exist only as long as the tooth exists. Rust on a car and a decaying carcass illustrate the same point. Evil exists as a corruption of something good; it is a privation and does not have essence by itself.[2] Norman Geisler tells us, "Evil is like a wound in an arm or moth-holes in a garment. It exists only in another but not in itself."[3]

Of course, to say that evil is not a thing in itself is not the same as saying that evil is unreal. Evil may not be an actual substance, but it involves an actual privation in good substances. Geisler notes, "It is not an actual entity but a real corruption in an actual entity."[4] Rotting trees, rusting cars, tooth decay, brain cancer, Greg's death—all these are examples of how evil is a corruption of something good.

It is one thing to understand what evil *is.* It is an entirely different thing to understand how such evil can exist in a world created by God. The problem of evil may be viewed in simple form as a conflict involving three concepts: *God's power, God's goodness,* and *the presence of evil in the world.* Common sense tells us that all three cannot be true at the same time.[5] Solutions to the problem of evil typically involve modifying one or more of these three concepts: *limit God's power, limit God's goodness,* or *modify the existence of evil* (such as calling it an illusion).[6]

Certainly if God made no claims to being good, then the existence of evil would be easier to explain. But God does claim to be good. If God were limited in power so that he was not strong enough to withstand evil, the existence of evil would be easier to explain. But God does claim to be all-powerful. If evil were just an illusion that had no reality, the problem wouldn't really exist in the first place. But evil is not an illusion. It is real.[7]

Today we face the reality of both *moral evil* (evil committed by free moral agents, involving such things as war, crime, cruelty, class struggles, discrimination, slavery, ethnic cleansing, suicide bombings, and various injustices) and *natural evil* (involving such things as hurricanes, floods, earthquakes, and the like). God is good, God is all-powerful, yet evil exists. This is the problem of evil in its most basic form.

Prominent thinkers like David Hume, H. G. Wells, and Bertrand Russell have concluded, on the basis of their observations of suffering and evil, that the God of the Bible does not exist.[8] Hume put it succinctly when he wrote of God, "Is he willing to prevent evil, but not able? Then he is impotent. Is he able, but not willing? Then he is malevolent. Is he both able and willing: whence then is evil?"[9] If there is a God—and he is *all-good* and *all-powerful*—then such atrocities as Hitler's murder of six million Jews never would have happened.

Certainly Christians agree that what Hitler did to the Jews was a horrible crime. But I must hasten to note, before offering a biblical viewpoint on the problem of evil, that the very act of categorizing Hitler's actions as evil raises an important philosophical point. As many thinkers have noted, if one is going to claim there is evil in the world, one must ask by what criteria something is judged to be evil in the first place.[10] How does one judge some things to be evil and other things not to be evil? What is the moral measuring stick by which people and events are morally appraised? By what process is evil distinguished from good and vice versa?

The reality is that it is impossible to distinguish evil from good unless one has an infinite reference point that is absolutely good.[11] Otherwise one is like a person on a boat at sea on a cloudy night without a compass (i.e., there would be no way to distinguish north from south without the absolute reference point of the compass needle).

The infinite reference point for distinguishing good from evil can be found only in the person of God, for God alone can exhaust the definition of "absolutely good." If God does not exist, then there are no moral absolutes by which one has the right to judge something (or someone) as being evil. More specifically, if God does not exist, there is no ultimate basis to judge, for example, the crimes of Hitler. Seen in this light, the reality of evil actually requires the existence of God rather than disproves it.

WHAT IS THE ORIGIN OF EVIL?

The original creation was "very good" (Genesis 1:31). There was no sin, no evil, no pain, and no death. Yet today the world is permeated with sin, evil, pain, and death. What brought these things about? Scripture indicates that the turn downward came the moment Adam and Eve used their God-given free will to choose to disobey God (see Genesis 3).

Some people wonder why God couldn't have created humans in such a way that we would never sin, thus avoiding evil altogether. The fact is, such a scenario would mean that we were not truly human. We would not have the capacity to make choices and to freely love. This scenario would require that God create robots who would act only in programmed ways— like a chatty doll whose string you pull and it says, "I love you."[12] Paul Little notes that with such a doll "there would never be any hot words, never any conflict, never anything said or done that would make you sad! But who would want that? There would never be any love either. Love is voluntary. God could have made us like robots, but we would have ceased to be men. God apparently thought it worth the risk of creating us as we are."[13]

Love cannot be programmed; it must be freely expressed. God wanted Adam and all humanity to show love by freely choosing obedience. This is why God gave Adam and all other humans a free will. Geisler is correct in saying that "forced love is rape; and God is not a divine rapist. He will not do anything to coerce their decision."[14] A *free* choice, however, leaves the possibility of a *wrong* choice. As J. B. Phillips put it, "Evil is inherent in the risky gift of free will."[15]

In view of the scriptural facts, we may conclude that God's plan had the potential for evil when he bestowed on humans the freedom of choice, but the actual origin of evil came as a result of a man who directed his will away from God and toward his own selfish desires.[16] Norman Geisler and Jeff Amanu note, "Whereas God created the *fact* of freedom, humans perform the *acts* of freedom. God made evil possible; creatures make it actual."[17] Ever since Adam and Eve made evil actual on that first occasion in the Garden of Eden, a sin nature has been passed on to every man and woman (see Romans 5:12; 1 Corinthians 15:22), and it is out of the sin nature that we today continue to use our free will to make evil actual (see Mark 7:20–23).

Even natural evil—involving earthquakes, tornadoes, floods, and the like—is rooted in our wrong use of free choice. We must not forget that we are living in a fallen world, and because of this, we are subject to disasters in the world of nature that would not have occurred had man not rebelled against God in the beginning (see Romans 8:20–22).[18] The Garden of Eden had no natural disasters or death until after the sin of Adam and Eve (see Genesis 1–3). There will be no natural disasters or death in the new heavens and earth when God puts an end to evil once and for all (see Revelation 21:4).[19]

WHAT IS GOD'S ULTIMATE PURPOSE IN ALLOWING EVIL?

The fact that humans used God-given free choice to disobey God did not take God by surprise. C. S. Lewis suggests that God in his omniscience "saw that from a world of free creatures, even though they fell, he could work out . . . a deeper happiness and a fuller splendor than any world of automata would admit."[20] Or, as Geisler has put it so well, the theist does not have to claim that our present world is the best of all possible worlds, but it is the best way *to* the best possible world:

> If God is to both preserve freedom and defeat evil, then this is the best way to do it. Freedom is preserved in that each person makes his own free choice to determine his destiny. Evil is overcome in that, once those who reject God are separated from the others, the decisions of all are made permanent. Those who choose God will be confirmed in it, and sin will cease. Those who reject God are in eternal quarantine and cannot upset the perfect world that has come about. The ultimate goal of a perfect world with free creatures will have been achieved, but the way to get there requires that those who abuse their freedom be cast out.[21]

A critically important factor involved in the suggestion that this may not be the best possible world but it is the best way *to* the best possible world is that *God is not finished yet.* Too often people fall into the trap of thinking that because God hasn't dealt with evil yet, he is not dealing with it at all. My old colleague Walter Martin used to say, "I've read the last chapter in the book, and we win!" Evil will one day be done away with. Just because evil is not destroyed right now does not mean it never will be.

In view of the above facts, the existence of evil in the world is seen to be compatible with the existence of an all-good and all-powerful God. We can summarize the facts this way:

1.   If God is all-good, he will defeat evil.
2.   If God is all-powerful, he can defeat evil.
3.   Evil is not yet defeated.
4.   Therefore, God can and will one day defeat evil.[22]

One day in the future, Christ will return, strip away power from the wicked, and hold all men and women accountable for the things they did during their time on earth (see Matthew 25:31–46; Revelation 20:11–15). Justice will ultimately prevail. Those who enter eternity without having trusted in Jesus Christ for salvation will understand just how effectively God has dealt with the problem of evil.

Some Inadequate Solutions to the Problem of Evil

WOULDN'T IT BE BETTER IF GOD DID AWAY WITH ALL EVIL IMMEDIATELY?

Some skeptics may be tempted to rebut that it should not take all of human history for an omnipotent God to deal with the problem of evil. God certainly has the option of doing away with all evil immediately— but choosing this option would have definite and fatal implications for each of us. As Paul Little has pointed out, "If God were to stamp out evil today, he would do a complete job. His action would have to include our lies and personal impurities, our lack of love, and our failure to do good. Suppose God were to decree that at midnight tonight all evil would be removed from the universe—who of us would still be here after midnight?"[23]

Even though God's ultimate solution to the problem of evil awaits the future, as I have argued, God has even now taken steps to ensure that evil doesn't run utterly amok. Indeed, God has given us human government to withstand lawlessness (see Romans 13:1–7). God founded the church to be a light in the midst of the darkness, to strengthen God's people, and even to help restrain the growth of wickedness in the world through the power of the Holy Spirit (e.g., Acts 16:5; 1 Timothy 3:15). In his Word God has given us a moral standard to guide us and keep us on the right path (see Psalm 119). He has given us the family unit to bring stability to society (e.g., Proverbs 22:15; 23:13). And much more![24]

DOES THE EXISTENCE OF EVIL PROVE THAT GOD IS FINITE?

Finite godism was popularized in the early 1980s by Rabbi Harold Kushner, author of the best-selling book *When Bad Things Happen to Good People*. In wrestling with the premature death of his son, Kushner concluded that God wants the righteous to live happy lives, but sometimes he cannot bring it about. There are some things God simply cannot control. God is good, but he is not powerful enough to bring about all the good things he desires. In short, God is finite. Kushner writes, "I recognize His limitations. He is limited in what He can do by the laws of nature and by the evolution of human nature and human moral freedom."[25] He laments that "even God has a hard time keeping chaos in check and limiting the damage that evil can do."[26]

Finite godism espouses a God who, because he is finite, can only be a contingent being who himself needs a cause. Such a God is not worthy of our worship. Nor is this God worthy of our trust, for there is no guarantee that he will be able to defeat evil in the future.

Finitism fails to consider that God's timing is not human timing. As noted previously, the fact that God has not defeated evil today does not mean he is not eliminating it in the future (see 2 Peter 3:7–12; Revelation 20–22). This is not the best of all possible worlds, but it is the best way to the best of all possible worlds.

Finitism clearly goes against the biblical testimony of God. Scripture portrays God as being *omnipotent*—meaning that he is all-powerful. He has the power to do all that he desires and wills. Some fifty-six times Scripture declares that God is *almighty* (e.g., Revelation 19:6).[27] God is abundant in strength (see Psalm 147:5) and has incomparably great power (see 2 Chronicles 20:6; Ephesians 1:19–21). No one can hold back God's hand (see Daniel 4:35). No one can reverse God's actions (see Isaiah 43:13), and no one can thwart him (see Isaiah 14:27). Nothing is impossible with God (see Matthew 19:26; Mark 10:27; Luke 1:37), and nothing is too difficult for him (see Genesis 18:14; Jeremiah 32:17, 27). The Almighty reigns (see Revelation 19:6), and he will one day overthrow all evil.

IS EVIL JUST AN ILLUSION?

Some people, particularly those affiliated with the Mind Sciences, argue that evil is an illusion. Mary Baker Eddy, the founder of Christian Science, argued that matter, evil, sickness, and death are unreal and are illusions of the mortal mind.[28] Unity School of Christianity writer Emily Cady likewise wrote, "There is no evil. . . . Pain, sickness, poverty, old age, and death are not real, and they have no power over me."[29] Ernest Holmes, founder of Religious Science, wrote, "All apparent evil is the result of ignorance, and will disappear to the degree that it is no longer thought about, believed in, or indulged in."[30]

If evil is just an illusion, however, then why fight it? Even though Mary Baker Eddy said the evils of bodily sickness and death are illusions, it is a historical fact that in her declining years she was under a doctor's care, received morphine injections to ease her pain, wore eyeglasses, had teeth extractions, and eventually died, thus "giving the lie" to all she professed to believe and teach.[31]

When people claim that evil is an illusion, I think it is fair game to ask them if they lock their front door at night. (If they do, ask them why.) Do they leave their key in the ignition when the car is parked downtown on Main Street? (If not, why not?) Do they buckle their seat belts in the car? (Why?) Do they go to the dentist? (Why? Tooth pain is an illusion, right?)

Do they put life vests on their little children when they swim in the ocean? (Why?) Do they warn their little children not to get too close to the fire at the cookout? (Why?) Do they support laws against pedophiles? (Why?) If evil is an illusion, then such things are completely unnecessary and should be of no concern to anyone.

The "illusion explanation" for evil flies in the face of all human experience and reason. Simply denying that evil exists does not negate its reality. This explanation of evil is in itself delusional thinking at its worst. Jesus certainly believed in the reality of evil. In the Lord's Prayer, he did not teach us to pray "Deliver us from the illusion of evil," but "Deliver us from evil."

For us to accept the view of Christian Science that evil is an illusion, we would have to deny our own senses and personal experiences. It is worth noting that Scripture often exhorts us to pay attention to empirical evidence by using our five senses. Jesus told doubting Thomas to stick his fingers into Jesus' crucifixion wounds as a way of proving to Thomas that indeed Jesus had risen from the dead (see John 20:27). In Luke 24:39 the resurrected Jesus told his followers, "Look at my hands and my feet. It is I myself! Touch me and see; a ghost does not have flesh and bones, as you see I have." We read in 1 John 1:1 that John and the apostles spoke of that "which we have heard, which we have seen with our eyes, which we have looked at and our hands have touched—this we proclaim concerning the Word of life." The same senses that so convincingly testify to the resurrected Christ testify to the reality of evil in our world—not just to a few people, but universally and throughout all ages.

CAN NEW AGE PANTHEISM ACCOUNT FOR EVIL?

I have a friend, Jim, who has read a few of my books on apologetics and the New Age movement. He developed a particular physical ailment one day and went to see a doctor who had been recommended to him. About halfway through the exam, Jim started to suspect that this doctor might be an advocate of New Age medicine. So Jim—not known for beating around the bush—blurted out, "Are you god?" To which the doctor exuberantly replied, "Why, yes, and so are you and everyone else." Jim was out of that office faster than greased lightning.

Pantheism is the view that God is all and all is God. The word *pantheism* comes from two Greek words—*pan* ("all") and *theos* ("God"). In pantheism all reality is viewed as being infused with divinity. The god of New Age pantheism is an impersonal, amoral "it" as opposed to the personal, moral "he" of Christianity. The distinction between the Creator and the creation is completely obliterated in this view.

If it is true that "all is one" and "all is God," as the New Age worldview holds, the distinction between good and evil ultimately disappears. New Ager David Spangler affirms that New Age ethics "is not based on . . . dualistic concepts of 'good' and 'bad.'"[32] There are no absolute moral wrongs and no absolute moral rights. Everything is relative. Of course, philosophers have long pointed out the philosophical weakness of such a viewpoint, for it amounts to saying that it is an absolute truth that there are no absolutes. When a New Ager tells me there are no absolutes, I always ask him if he is absolutely sure about that.

A major problem with the New Age pantheistic worldview is that it fails to adequately deal with the existence of real evil in the world. If God is the essence of all life-forms in creation, one must conclude that both good and evil stem from the same essence (God). In other words, such things as World War I and II, Hitler, murder, cancer, rape, and other manifestations of evil are a part of God.

The Bible, by contrast, teaches that God is good and not evil (see 1 Chronicles 16:34; Psalm 118:29; 136:1; 145:8–9; Matthew 19:17). The God of the Bible is light, and "in him there is no darkness at all" (see 1 John 1:5; cf. Habakkuk 1:13; Matthew 5:48). First John 1:5 is particularly cogent in the Greek, which translates literally: "And darkness there is not in him, not in any way." John could not have said it more forcefully.

I had the opportunity to converse with former guru Rabi Maharaj, and he spoke at length of the ethical dissatisfaction he felt regarding a monistic, pantheistic worldview, especially as it pertained to the problem of evil.

My growing awareness of God as the Creator, separate and distinct from the universe he had made, contradicted the Hindu concept that God was everything, that the Creator and the Creation were one and the same. If there was only One Reality, then [God] was evil as well as good, death as well as life, hatred as well as love. That made everything meaningless, life an absurdity. It was not easy to maintain both one's sanity and the view that good and evil, love and hate, life and death were One Reality.[33]

Rabi made the only logical choice and became a Christian!

DO WE CREATE OUR OWN REALITIES?

Many New Agers believe that people create *all* their own realities—both good *and* bad—by the power of the mind. Popular New Age writers David Gershon and Gail Straub note that "we can't avoid creating our reality; each time we think a thought we are creating it. Every belief we hold is shaping what we experience in our life."[34] In view of this, "If we accept the basic premise that our thoughts create our reality, it means that we need to take responsibility for creating *all* of our reality—the parts we like and the parts we don't like."[35]

A critical problem with this view is that if humans (as gods) create their own reality, as New Agers argue, then one cannot condemn individuals who inflict evil on others. For example, one must conclude that the millions of Jews who were executed under Hitler's regime created their own reality. Hence, Hitler's actions cannot be condemned as ethically wrong, since Hitler was only part of a reality that the Jews themselves created. Similarly, one cannot condemn terrorists who blow up passenger jets, because the people on these jets create their own reality.

When the acting teacher of Shirley MacLaine's daughter was burned beyond recognition in a head-on collision, MacLaine wondered, "Why did she choose to die that way?"[36] Christian apologist Douglas Groothuis, after reading MacLaine's book *It's All in the Playing,* recounts how in the book "we find Shirley sobbing in front of her television set when she sees the effects of a Chilean volcano that killed 25,000 people. Why cry? They chose that death, didn't they?"[37]

The more one ponders this New Age explanation of evil, the more absurd it gets.

DOES REINCARNATION EXPLAIN THE EXISTENCE OF EVIL?

Many New Agers base their ethics on reincarnation and karma. The process of reincarnation (continual rebirths) is said to continue until the soul has reached a state of perfection and merges back with its source (God or the Universal Soul). Karma refers to the "debt" a soul accumulates because of good or bad actions committed during one's life (or past lives). If one accumulates good karma, he or she will allegedly be reincarnated in a desirable state. If one accumulates bad karma, he or she will be reincarnated in a less desirable state.

Many New Agers explain the existence of evil in our world strictly in terms of karma. Popular New Age writer Gary Zukav, for example, says we must not presume to judge when people suffer cruelly, for "we do not know what is being healed [via karma] in these sufferings."[38] What Zukav calls "nonjudgmental justice" relieves us of having to be judge and jury regarding apparent evil; the law of karma will bring about justice in the end.

Would Zukav really have us believe that when soldiers in Ceylon shot a nursing mother and then shot off the toes of her baby for target practice, this was somehow bringing "healing" to her and her child's souls? When Shiites in the Soviet Union ripped open the womb of a pregnant Armenian woman and tore the limbs from the fetus (real events reported in the newspaper), does Zukav really expect us to place our faith in "nonjudgmental justice" instead of becoming morally outraged? Where is the divine and the sacred in this?

There are numerous problems with the doctrine of reincarnation. Practically speaking, one must ask, Why does one get punished for something he or she cannot remember having done in a previous life? Further, if (as we are told) the purpose of karma is to rid humanity of its selfish desires over many lifetimes, then why has there not been a noticeable improvement in human nature after all the millennia of reincarnations? Why has evil continued to grow? Still further, if reincarnation and the law of karma are so beneficial on a practical level, as New Agers claim, then how do they explain the continued social and economic problems— including widespread poverty, starvation, disease, and horrible suffering— in India, where reincarnation has been systematically taught throughout its history?

Certainly reincarnation is unbiblical, going against what Scripture teaches about death and the afterlife. Hebrews 9:27 flatly asserts that "man is destined to die once, and after that to face judgment." Each human being lives once as a mortal on earth, dies once, and then faces judgment. He or she does not have a second chance by reincarnating into another body (see Luke 16:19–31; 2 Corinthians. 5:8).

Trusting God in a World of Suffering

There are other inadequate explanations for the problem of evil we could examine, but they are not as prominent today, and space forbids further exploration.[39]

Having earlier established that the existence of evil is in fact compatible with the existence of an all-good and all-powerful God, it is fitting to close by emphasizing that our loving heavenly Father calls us to trust him with childlike faith as we live in this world of suffering. Sometimes, as a parent, I have to make a decision for my son or daughter that may involve a little pain (like paying a visit to the dentist). From their perspective, they may not fully understand why I insist on this visit. I assure them that, despite the discomfort (and even pain), it is in their best interest to go to the dentist.

Sometimes we humans wonder why God allows us to go through certain painful circumstances. But just because we find it difficult to imagine what reasons God could have does not mean that no such reason exists. From our finite human perspective, we are often only able to see a few threads of the great tapestry of life and of the will of God. We do not have the full picture. That is why God calls us to trust him (see Hebrews 11). God sees the full picture and does not make mistakes. He has a reason for allowing painful circumstances to come our way—even if we cannot grasp it.

Geisler gives us something important to think about in this regard: Even in our finiteness, it is possible for humans to discover some good purposes for pain—such as warning us of greater evil (an infant need only touch a hot stove once to learn not to do it again), and to keep us from self-destruction (our built-in nerve endings detect pain so we won't, for example, continue to hold a hot pan in our hands). If finite humans can discover some good purposes for evil, then surely an infinitely wise God has a good purpose for all suffering.[40] We may not understand that purpose in the temporal "now," but it nonetheless exists. Our inability to discern why bad things sometimes happen to us does not disprove God's benevolence; it merely exposes our ignorance.[41]

It is good to keep in mind the dimension of time. Just as we evaluate a trip to the dentist in the light of the long-range benefits of such a visit, Scripture admonishes Christians to evaluate present sufferings in the light of eternity. As the apostle Paul observed, "I consider that our present sufferings are not worth comparing with the glory that will be revealed in us" (Romans 8:18; see also 2 Corinthians 4:17; Hebrews 12:2; 1 Peter 1:6–7).[42]

And let us not forget that even when we encounter suffering, God has the ability as the sovereign Ruler of the universe to bring good out of it (see Romans 8:28). An example of this is the life of Joseph. His brothers were wrongly jealous of him (see Genesis 37:11), hated him (37:4, 5, 8), wanted to murder him (37:20), cast him into a pit (37:24), and sold him into slavery (37:28). Yet later Joseph could say to his brothers, "It was to save lives that God sent me ahead of you" (45:5), and "You intended to harm me, but God intended it for good to accomplish what is now being done, the saving of many lives" (50:20). Even though evil things happened to Joseph, God had a providential purpose in allowing them.

The apostle Paul certainly didn't like being imprisoned, but God had a providential purpose in allowing it to happen. After all, while in prison Paul wrote Ephesians, Philippians, Colossians, and Philemon (see Ephesians

3:1; Philippians 1:7; Colossians 4:10; and Philemon 9). God very clearly brought good out of Paul's suffering.

Sometimes the "good" that God brings out of our suffering involves drawing us closer to him. Joni Eareckson Tada, who broke her neck in a swimming accident and became quadriplegic, said her tragedy drew her much closer to God. She's even quoted as saying she would rather be in a wheelchair with God than be able to walk without God.

Sometimes the "good" that God brings out of our suffering involves a positive change in our character. Peter refers to this when he says, "In this you greatly rejoice, though now for a little while you may have had to suffer grief in all kinds of trials. These have come so that your faith—of greater worth than gold, which perishes even though refined by fire—may be proved genuine and may result in praise, glory and honor when Jesus Christ is revealed" (1 Peter 1:6–7; modern paraphrase: "No pain, no gain").

All this is said with a view to emphasizing the need for faith in the midst of this world of suffering. God is most assuredly working out his purpose in our midst, and we must trust him! I like the way Gary Habermas and J. P. Moreland put it. They encourage us to maintain a "top-down" perspective:

> The God of the universe invites us to view life and death from his eternal vantage point. And if we do, we will see how readily it can revolutionize our lives: daily anxieties, emotional hurts, tragedies, our responses and responsibilities to others, possessions, wealth, and even physical pain and death. All of this and much more can be informed and influenced by the truths of heaven. The repeated witness of the New Testament is that believers should view all problems, indeed, their entire existence, from what we call the "top-down" perspective: God and his kingdom first, followed by various aspects of our earthly existence.[43]

At the beginning of the chapter, I mentioned my brother's son Greg, who tragically died. I must tell you that the one thing that has sustained the entire family is a top-down perspective. In the future—when we finally reach the "best of all possible worlds" that God is bringing about, that

heavenly country "whose architect and builder is God" (Hebrews 11:10)—
we will have a grand reunion that will never end! Death, evil, pain, and
tears will be a thing of the distant past.

QUESTIONS FOR REFLECTION AND DISCUSSION

1. Explain why "it is impossible to distinguish evil from good unless one has an infinite reference point that is absolutely good."

2. What does the author mean when he argues, "The theist does not have to claim that our present world is the best of all possible worlds, but it is the best way *to* the best possible world"?

3. How might a top-down perspective help you wrestle with evil and suffering? How do you think you go about acquiring such a perspective?

Chapter 3

TOUGH QUESTIONS ABOUT SCIENCE

WILLIAM LANE CRAIG

B ack in 1896 the president of Cornell University, Andrew Dickson White, published a book titled *A History of the Warfare of Science with Theology in Christendom*.[1] Under White's influence, the metaphor of warfare to describe the relations between science and the Christian faith became widespread during the first half of the twentieth century. The culturally dominant view in our society—even among Christians—came to be that science and Christianity are not *allies* in the search for truth, but *adversaries*. To illustrate, a few years ago I agreed to participate in a debate with a philosopher of science at Simon Fraser University in Vancouver on the question "Are Science and Religion Mutually Irrelevant?" But when I walked onto the campus, I saw that the Christian students sponsoring the debate had advertised it with large banners and posters proclaiming "Science vs. Christianity." The Christian students were perpetuating the same sort of warfare mentality that Andrew Dickson White proclaimed a hundred years earlier.

ARE SCIENCE AND CHRISTIANITY ALLIES OR ADVERSARIES?

What happened, however, during the second half of the twentieth century was that historians and philosophers of science came to realize that this supposed history of warfare is a myth. As Charles Thaxton and Nancy Pearcey point out in their book *The Soul of Science*,[2] for more than three hundred years between the rise of modern science in the 1500s and the late 1800s, the relationship between science and religion can best be described as an alliance. White's book is now regarded as something of a bad joke, a one-sided and distorted piece of propaganda. Today it is cited only as an example of how *not* to do history of science.

Historians of science now recognize the indispensable role played by the Christian faith in the rise and development of modern science. Science is not something that is natural to humankind. As science writer Loren Eiseley has emphasized, science is "an invented cultural institution" that requires a "unique soil" in order to flourish.[3] Modern science did not arise in the Orient or in Africa, but in Western civilization. Why is this so? It is due to the unique contribution of the Christian faith to Western culture. As Eiseley states, "It is the Christian world which finally gave birth in a clear, articulate fashion to the experimental method of science itself."[4]

In contrast to Eastern religions and folk religions, Christianity does not view the world as divine or as indwelt by spirits, but rather as the natural product of a transcendent creator who designed and brought it into being. Thus, the world is a rational place that is open to exploration and discovery. Up until the late 1800s, scientists were typically Christian believers who saw no conflict between their science and their faith—men like Kepler, Boyle, Maxwell, Faraday, Kelvin, and others. The idea of a warfare between science and religion is a relatively recent invention of the late nineteenth century, a myth carefully nurtured by secular thinkers who had as their aim the undermining of the cultural dominance of Christianity and its replacement by naturalism—the view that nothing outside nature is real and the only way to discover truth is through science. They were remarkably successful in pushing through their agenda.

But philosophers of science during the second half of the twentieth century came to realize that the whole scientific enterprise is based on certain assumptions that cannot be proved scientifically, but that *are* guaranteed by the Christian worldview: for example, the laws of logic, the orderly nature of the external world, the reliability of our cognitive faculties in knowing the world, the validity of inductive reasoning, and the objectivity of the moral values used in science. I want to emphasize that science could not even exist without these assumptions, and yet these assumptions cannot be proved scientifically. They are philosophical assumptions, which, interestingly, are part and parcel of a Christian worldview. Thus, theology is an ally to science in that it can furnish a conceptual framework in which science can exist. More than that, the Christian religion historically furnished the conceptual framework in which modern science was born and nurtured.

We are thus now living in an era of renewed interest in the relations between science and Christian theology. Indeed, during the last quarter of the twentieth century, a flourishing dialogue between science and theology has been going on in North America and Europe. Numerous societies for promoting this dialogue have sprung up: the European Society for the Study of Science and Theology, the Science and Religion Forum, the Center for Theology and Natural Science (CTNS), and so forth. Especially significant have been the ongoing conferences sponsored by the CTNS and the Vatican Observatory, in which prominent scientists like Stephen Hawking and Paul Davies have explored the implications of science for theology with prominent theologians like John Polkinghorne and Wolfhart Pannenberg. Not only are there professional journals devoted to the dialogue between science and religion, such as *Zygon* and *Perspectives on Science and Christian Faith,* but, more significantly, secular journals like *Nature* and the *British Journal for the Philosophy of Science* also carry articles on the mutual implications of science and theology. The dialogue between science and theology has become so significant in our day that both Cambridge University and Oxford University have moved to establish chairs in science and theology. I say all this simply to counteract a cultural myth, a myth that is rooted in ignorance and rejected by most scholars today—the myth that science and Christian faith are inherently adversaries rather than allies in the quest for truth.

HOW SHOULD THEOLOGY AND SCIENCE RELATE?

Answers to this much-discussed question basically divide into two broad camps: those who insist that no conflict between science and theology is possible and those who see such conflict as possible. Christians should beware of accepting the easy answer of the first camp. It is very tempting for religious believers to try to avoid the whole problem by asserting that science and religion cannot come into conflict, so why worry about it? But this answer can be seen to be unacceptable once we examine it closely. For anyone who opts for this first answer must espouse either a *double-truth theory,* according to which something can be scientifically false but theologically true, or else *complementarianism,* the view that science and theology are two nonoverlapping domains (science tells us facts, and theology gives us value and meaning). But the double-truth theory is incoherent, since there is objective truth about the way reality is. (To say "There is no objective truth" is to assert a purportedly objective truth and so is self-refuting!) But if there is objective truth about the way the world is, it makes no sense to assert, for example, that while it is scientifically true that the universe is eternal and uncreated, nevertheless, it is theologically true that it had a beginning and was created.

As for complementarianism, this popular approach is all too often a thinly veiled excuse for disregarding religious truth claims—as evident in Freeman Dyson's candid remark, "When all is said and done, science is about things, and theology is about words."[5] But complementarianism is also unacceptable, because the Christian faith makes historical assertions, and history is epistemologically on a par with science, as is especially evident in such historical sciences as paleontology and cosmology. Therefore, one cannot avoid the possibility of conflicting truth claims in science and religion. This is admittedly risky for the Christian faith: It puts its truth on the line. But it also makes Christianity great because the same common world that makes conflict possible also affords the possibility of verification of Christian theology's truth claims.

HOW DOES MODERN SCIENCE DESCRIBE THE WORLD?

C. P. Snow lamented in his famous essay "The Two Cultures" that most people living in a scientific age and enjoying daily the benefits of modern science still do not have a clue as to what science teaches us about the world.[6] Even though most of us have had science classes throughout elementary school and high school, few could describe even in its broad strokes the picture of the world painted by modern science. But without an understanding of how contemporary science sees the world, it will be impossible for us to relate our theology to it and so arrive at a unified worldview. Therefore, with the help of Victor Weisskopf,[7] allow me to sketch the contours of the modern scientific view of the world as it has developed historically:

1. Unification of Celestial and Terrestrial Mechanics: The same laws of nature hold throughout the universe.

2. Existence of Atomic Species: All matter is the result of combining around a hundred different kinds of atoms.

3. Heat as Random Motion: Heat is due to motion of material particles and is not itself a substance.

4. Unification of Electricity, Magnetism, and Optics: All these are manifestations of the electromagnetic field.

5. Evolution of Living Species: Life and biological complexity arose as described by the neo-Darwinian synthesis.

6. Relativity Theory: Space and time are unified into four-dimensional space-time, whose curvature corresponds to gravitational fields.

7. Quantum Theory: There are limits on the subatomic level to classical notions like position and momentum due to the causal indeterminacy.

8. Molecular Biology: The discovery of the DNA macro-molecule revealed the genetic code responsible for the development of living species.

9. Quantum "Ladder": Material systems are hierarchically ordered such that the smaller the system the greater the energy packed into it, thus unlocking the secret of nuclear energy.

10. Expanding Universe: The universe has an evolutionary history that began in the Big Bang.

Important questions of apologetic significance arise in many of these areas. Alert Christians, especially Christian leaders, need to have some general understanding of these issues and be prepared to offer a perspective on them and direct inquirers to appropriate resources for more in-depth answers. Unfortunately, there are so many issues to discuss and the topics are so vast that we can't even scratch the surface in the space allotted here. Therefore, I've chosen to address briefly just four areas of significant recent interaction between Christian theology and science.

WHERE DID THE UNIVERSE COME FROM?

Point 10 of the contours of the scientific worldview raises the issue of cosmic origins. It is the ultimate question of creation: Where did the universe come from? Why does it exist? The Bible begins with the words, "In the beginning God created the heavens and the earth." The Bible thus teaches that the universe had a beginning. It does not teach that this beginning was recent. That is a mistaken inference based on adding up the life spans of various Old Testament figures. But the Old Testament genealogies do not purport to record every generation, and in any case, such a reckoning would take us back only as far as the creation of life on earth (Genesis 1:2), not to the very origin of the universe (Genesis 1:1). From ancient times until the twentieth century the biblical doctrine that the universe had a beginning has been repudiated by both Greek philosophy and modern atheism. In spite of this, the church has stood firm in its affirmation of the temporal creation of the universe from nothing.

Then in 1929 an alarming thing happened. A scientist named Edwin Hubble discovered that the light from distant galaxies appears to be redder than it should be. The startling conclusion to which Hubble was led is that the light is redder because the universe is growing apart—it is expanding! Therefore, the light from the galaxies is affected, since they are moving away from us.

This is the interesting part: Hubble not only showed that the universe is expanding but that it is expanding the same in all directions. To get a picture of this, imagine a balloon with buttons glued on it. As you blow up the balloon, the buttons get farther and farther apart, even though they are stuck in place. These buttons are just like the galaxies in space. As space itself expands, all the galaxies in the universe grow farther and farther apart.

The staggering implication is that, as we go back in time, everything was closer and closer together. Ultimately, at some point in the finite past, the entire known universe was contracted down to a mathematical point, which scientists call the "singularity," from which it has been expanding ever since. The farther back one goes in the past, the denser the universe becomes, so that one finally reaches a point of infinite density from which the universe began to expand. This initial event has come to be known as the "Big Bang."

This event that marked the beginning of the universe becomes all the more amazing when one reflects on the fact that nothing existed before it. Nothing existed prior to the singularity, for it is the edge of physical space and time. It therefore represents the origin, not only of all matter and energy, but also of physical space and time themselves. Physicists John Barrow and Frank Tipler observe, "At this singularity, space and time came into existence; literally nothing existed before the singularity, so, if the Universe originated at such a singularity, we would truly have a creation out of nothing."[8]

Such a conclusion is profoundly disturbing for anyone who ponders it. For the question cannot be suppressed: Why does *the universe* exist rather than nothing? There can be no natural, physical cause of the Big Bang event, since, in philosopher Quentin Smith's words, "It belongs analytically to the concept of the cosmological singularity that it is not the effect of prior physical events. The definition of a singularity . . . entails that it is impossible to extend the spacetime manifold beyond the singularity. . . . This rules out the idea that the singularity is an effect of some prior natural process."[9] Sir Arthur Eddington, contemplating the beginning of the universe, opined that the expansion of the universe was so preposterous and incredible that "I feel almost an indignation that anyone should believe in it—except myself."[10] He finally felt forced to conclude, "The beginning seems to present insuperable difficulties unless we agree to look on it as frankly supernatural."[11]

Some people were understandably disturbed by the idea that the universe appeared to have been created from nothing. So they tried to find ways to avert the initial singularity and regain an eternal universe—but all in vain. The history of twentieth-century cosmology has been the history of the repeated falsification of such nonstandard theories and the corroboration of the Big Bang theory.[12] It has been the overwhelming verdict of the scientific community that none of these alternative theories are superior to the Big Bang theory. Again and again models aimed at averting the prediction of the standard model of an absolute beginning of the universe have been shown to be either untenable or not to avert the beginning after all. For example, in some such theories, like the oscillating universe (which expands and contracts forever) or the chaotic inflationary universe (which continually spawns new universes), while the universes posited do have a potentially infinite future, they turn out to have only a finite past. Vacuum fluctuation universe theories (which postulate an eternal vacuum out of which our universe is born) cannot explain why, if the vacuum was eternal, we do not observe an infinitely old universe. Though still bandied about in the popular press, such models have been abandoned by almost all theorists today.

One of the most celebrated recent attempts to avoid the initial singularity comes from Stephen Hawking's quantum gravity theory, which has received a great deal of attention in the popular press through his best-selling book *A Brief History of Time*. In Hawking's theory, the past is finite but doesn't have any beginning point or edge. Hawking is not at all reluctant to draw theological implications from his model. He writes, "The universe would have neither beginning nor end and would be neither created nor destroyed. It would just be. What place, then, for a creator?"[13]

Unfortunately for detractors of creation, Hawking's model cannot be a realistic description of the universe. To mention just one point: Hawking presupposes that the universe exists in imaginary time instead of real time. This means that in his equations Hawking uses imaginary numbers for the time coordinate, numbers like $\sqrt{-1}$. The problem is that such numbers are just mathematical devices or tricks that have no physical meaning. Way back in 1920 Eddington explored what he called the "dodge" of using imaginary numbers for the time coordinate, but he thought it was "not very profitable" to speculate on the implications of this, for, he said, "it can scarcely be regarded as anything more than an analytical device."[14] Imaginary time, he said, was merely an illustrative tool, which "certainly does not correspond to any physical reality."[15]

Remarkably, in his more recent book, *The Nature of Space and Time* (1996), Hawking admits this. He says, "A physical theory is just a mathematical model and it is meaningless to ask whether it corresponds to reality. . . . All I'm concerned with is that the theory should predict the results of measurements."[16] But if that is all Hawking's theory does, then it obviously does not eliminate either the real beginning of the universe or the need for a creator. It is simply a mathematical way of redescribing a universe with a singular beginning in such a way that the singularity does not appear in the redescription. In any case, Hawking's theory, if interpreted realistically, still involves an absolute origin of the universe, even if the universe does not begin in a singularity, as it does in the standard Big Bang theory.[17] His model lacks a beginning *point,* but it has only a finite past and therefore an absolute origin. Hawking himself sums up the situation: "Almost everyone now believes that the universe, and time itself, had a beginning at the Big Bang."[18]

Given the obvious theological implications of the origin of the universe from nothing, we can expect that alternative theories to the Big Bang model, which attempt to restore an eternal universe, will continue to be proposed. Paul Steinhardt of Princeton University has recently received a great deal of coverage in the popular press for his new cyclic/ekpyrotic model of the universe.[19] Such proposed alternatives are to be welcomed and evaluated by the evidence, for if the pattern of failure of such alternatives continues, the prediction of an absolute beginning by the standard Big Bang model will be further corroborated, thereby gaining in credibility. Despite many people's predisposition to the contrary, the accumulating evidence has consistently supported the view that the universe was created out of nothing. J. M. Wersinger, professor of physics at Auburn University, makes these observations:

At first the scientific community was very reluctant to accept the idea of a birth of the universe.

Not only did the Big Bang model seem to give in to the Judeo-Christian idea of a beginning of the world, but it also seemed to call for an act of supernatural creation. . . .

It took time, observational evidence, and careful verification of predictions made by the Big Bang model to convince the scientific community to accept the idea of a cosmic genesis.

. . . the Big Bang is a very successful model that imposed itself on a reluctant scientific community.[20]

Against all expectation, science thus verified the Bible's prediction of the beginning of the universe.

WHAT DOES THE FINE-TUNING OF THE UNIVERSE MEAN?

The fact that the universe exists is no guarantee that it will be life-permitting. Scientists once thought that whatever the initial conditions of the universe were, eventually the universe would evolve the complex life-forms we see today, as mentioned in point 5 of the contours of a scientific view of the world (see page 53). One of the newest findings concerning the origin and evolution of life, however, has been the discovery of how incredibly fine-tuned our universe had to be right from the moment of the Big Bang in order for life to originate anywhere at all in the cosmos. During the last thirty years or so, scientists have been stunned by the discovery of how complex and sensitive a balance of initial conditions must be given in the Big Bang in order for the universe to permit the origin and evolution of life. In the various fields of physics and astrophysics, classical cosmology, quantum mechanics, and biochemistry, discoveries have repeatedly disclosed that the existence of life depends on a delicate balance of physical constants and quantities. If these were to be slightly altered, the balance would be destroyed and life would not exist. Indeed, in many cases, not even stars and planets, not even chemistry, not even atomic matter itself, would exist, much less biological life. In fact, the universe appears to have been incomprehensibly fine-tuned from the moment of its inception to permit the existence of intelligent life.

For example, changes in the gravitational force or the electromagnetic force by only one part in 10^{40} would have precluded the existence of stars like our sun, making life impossible. A decrease or increase in the speed of the expansion by only one part in a million million when the temperature of the universe was 10^{10} degrees would have either resulted in the universe's recollapse long ago into a hot fireball or precluded galaxies from ever condensing, in both cases making life impossible. The so-called cosmological constant, crucial to the development of our universe, must be inexplicably fine-tuned to an accuracy of one part in 10^{53} in order for a life-permitting universe to exist. These are just some of the many constants and quantities that must be fine-tuned if the universe is to be life-permitting.

And it's not just each quantity that must be fine-tuned, but their ratios to one another must also be finely tuned. Thus, the situation is not merely like all the roulette wheels in Monte Carlo turning up with a certain set of numbers; it is more like all the roulette wheels in Monte Carlo turning up with a certain set of numbers—and those numbers also having to stand in certain ratios to each other. For example, the number on one wheel must be seven times the number on another wheel and one-third the number on another wheel. It is overwhelmingly improbable that a life-permitting universe should exist.

How should we understand the notion of the probability of a life-permitting universe existing? John Barrow, a British physicist, gives us an idea.[21] He invites us to put a red dot on a piece of paper and let it represent our universe. Now vary some of the initial conditions just a hair, and let that represent a different universe. If it is life-permitting, put a red dot; if it is life-prohibiting, put a blue dot. Now do this again and again and again until the sheet of paper is covered with dots. Do you know what you wind up with? You get a sea of a blue with only a few pinpoints of red. It is in this sense that it can properly be said that the existence of a life-permitting universe is unbelievably improbable.

Sometimes people will say, "Yes, our universe is improbable. But any universe is equally improbable. It's like winning the lottery. Any particular person's winning it is highly improbable, but *somebody* has to win it." What this objection helps to bring out is that it is not just probability that is at stake here, but *specified* probability. It is not just the probability of one universe or another existing, but the probability of a *life-permitting* universe existing. Thus, the correct analogy would be a lottery in which a billion, billion, billion black balls were mixed together with one white ball, and you were invited to reach in blindfolded and pick out a ball. While every ball has an equal improbability of being picked, nevertheless, it is overwhelmingly more probable that whichever ball you pick, it will be black rather than white. To complete the analogy, imagine now that your life depended on the ball's being white; pick out a white ball, or you'll be killed! If you reached, blindfolded, into those jillions of black balls and discovered that you had pulled out the one and only white ball, you would rightly suspect that the whole thing was rigged. If you are still skeptical, imagine that in order to stave off execution you had to succeed in doing this three times in a row. The probabilities involved would not be significantly different, but you would be nuts if you thought you had accomplished this by chance.

WHAT DOES THE "MANY WORLDS" HYPOTHESIS MEAN?

Theorists who defend the alternative of chance have therefore been forced to adopt an extraordinary hypothesis: the "many worlds" hypothesis. According to this hypothesis, our universe is just one member of a greater collection of universes, all of which are real, actually existing universes, not merely possible universes. To ensure that somewhere in the world ensemble there will appear by chance a universe finely tuned for life, it is further stipulated that there are an infinite number of universes in the collection (so that every possibility will be realized) and that the physical constants and quantities are randomly ordered (so that the worlds are not all alike). Thus, somewhere in this world ensemble there will appear by chance alone finely tuned universes like ours. We should not be surprised to observe finely tuned conditions, since observers like us exist only in those universes that are finely tuned.

The fact that otherwise sober scientists should feel compelled to resort to such an extraordinary metaphysical hypothesis is a measure of the degree to which cosmic fine-tuning cries out for explanation. Paul Davies has recently declared that the case for design stands or falls with the success of the many worlds hypothesis.[22]

So what can be said of this hypothesis? First, we need to realize that it is no more scientific and no less metaphysical than a "cosmic designer" hypothesis. As the scientist-theologian John Polkinghorne says, "People try to trick out a 'many universe' account in sort of pseudo-scientific terms, but that is pseudo-science. It is a metaphysical guess that there might be many universes with different laws and circumstances."[23] But as a metaphysical hypothesis, the many worlds hypothesis is arguably inferior to the design hypothesis because the design hypothesis is *simpler*. According to a principle known as Ockham's Razor, we should not multiply causes beyond what is necessary to explain the effect. But it is simpler to postulate one cosmic designer to explain our universe than to postulate the infinitely bloated and contrived collection of universes required by the many worlds hypothesis. Therefore, the design hypothesis is to be preferred.

Second, there is no known way of generating a world ensemble. No one has been able to explain how or why such a varied collection of universes should exist. Moreover, the attempts that have been made require fine-tuning themselves. For example, although some cosmologists appeal to so-called inflationary theories of the universe to generate a world ensemble, the only consistent inflationary model is Linde's chaotic inflationary theory, and it requires fine-tuning to start the inflation.

Third, the many worlds hypothesis faces a severe challenge from "biological evolutionary" theory, which is one of the contours of the scientific worldview.[24] First, a bit of background: During the nineteenth century the German physicist Ludwig Boltzmann proposed a sort of many worlds hypothesis to explain why we do not find the universe in a state of "heat death" or thermodynamic equilibrium in which energy is evenly diffused throughout the universe.[25] Boltzmann hypothesized that the universe as a whole does, in fact, exist in an equilibrium state, but that over time fluctuations in the energy level occur here and there throughout the universe, so that by chance alone there will be isolated regions where disequilibrium exists. Boltzmann referred to these isolated regions as "worlds." We should not be surprised to see our world in a highly improbable disequilibrium state, since in the ensemble of all worlds there must exist by chance alone certain worlds in disequilibrium—and ours just happens to be one.

The problem with Boltzmann's daring many worlds hypothesis is that if our world is merely a fluctuation in a sea of diffuse energy, it is overwhelmingly more probable that we would be observing a much tinier region of disequilibrium than we do. For us to exist, a smaller fluctuation, even one that produced our world instantaneously by an enormous accident, is inestimably more probable than a progressive decline in entropy to fashion the world we see. In fact, Boltzmann's hypothesis, if adopted, would force us to regard the past as illusory—everything having the mere appearance of age—and the stars and planets as illusory. And that sort of world—in which stars are mere "pictures," as it were—is vastly more probable, given a state of overall equilibrium, than a world with genuine temporally and spatially distant events. Therefore, Boltzmann's many worlds hypothesis has been universally rejected by the scientific community, and the present disequilibrium is usually taken to be just a result of the initial low entropy condition mysteriously existing at the beginning of the universe.

Now a precisely parallel problem attends the many worlds hypothesis as an explanation of fine-tuning. According to the prevailing theory of biological evolution, intelligent life like ourselves, if it evolves at all, will do so as late in the lifetime of the sun as possible. The less the time span available for the mechanisms of genetic mutation and natural selection to function, the lower the probability of intelligent life evolving. Given the complexity of the human organism, it is overwhelmingly more probable that human beings will evolve late in the lifetime of the sun rather than early. Hence, if our universe is but one member of a world ensemble, it is overwhelmingly more probable that we should be observing a very old sun rather than a relatively young one of only a few billion years. If we are products of biological evolution, we should find ourselves in a world in which we evolve later in the lifetime of our star. In fact, adopting the many worlds hypothesis to explain away fine-tuning also results in a strange sort of illusionism. It is far more probable that all our astronomical, geological, and biological estimates of relatively young age are wrong, that we really do exist very late in the lifetime of the sun, and that the sun and Earth's appearance of youth is a massive illusion, which is sci-entifically crazy. Thus, either we are not chance products of biological evolu-tion (in which case design must be true) or else we are not chance products of a world ensemble (in which case design must be true). Either way we are led to a designer.

With the failure of the many worlds hypothesis, the last obstacle to the design inference concerning the fine-tuning of the universe falls away. Given the incomprehensible specified improbability of the initial condi-tions of the universe being fine-tuned for life, it is plausible to believe, as the Bible says, that this world has been providentially ordered by God to sus-tain life.

WHAT EXPLAINS THE ACTUAL ORIGIN OF LIFE?

The fine-tuning of the universe supplies certain prerequisites for the existence of life anywhere in the cosmos, but it does not guarantee that life actually will arise in the universe. In other words, while these finely tuned conditions are *necessary* conditions for life, they are not *sufficient* conditions for life. So, we may wonder, what else is needed? What explains the actual origin of life?

Most of us were probably taught in school that life originated in the so-called "primordial soup" by chance chemical reactions. Back in the 1950s, Stanley Miller was able to synthesize amino acids by passing electric sparks through methane gas. While amino acids are not alive, proteins are made out of amino acids—and proteins are found in living things—and so the hope was that somehow the origin of life could be explained.

On the face of it, such a scenario for life's origin seemed hopelessly improbable. Fred Hoyle and Chandra Wickramasinghe estimated that the odds against the required ten to twenty amino acids coming together by chance (remember that at this stage of the game there is no natural selection and so no chemical evolution) to form an enzyme is on the order of one chance out of 10^{20}. Given the size of the earth's oceans and the billions of years available, they thought such an improbability could be faced. But they point out that there are two thousand different enzymes made out of amino acids, all of which would have to be formed by chance, and the odds of that happening are around 1 in $10^{40,000}$, odds so "outrageously small" that they could not be faced "even if the whole universe consisted of organic soup."[26] And that is only the beginning. It still remains for DNA to arise from proteins and for the complex machinery of the cell to arise. These issues are too complex to set numbers to.

So the primordial soup scenario never had much going for it to begin with. What the average layperson doesn't realize, however, is that all of these old chemical "origin of life" scenarios have now broken down and been abandoned. This point has been wonderfully documented in the book *The Mystery of Life's Origin*.[27] The authors point out that there probably never was such a thing as the so-called primordial soup, because natural processes of destruction and dilution would have prevented the chemical reactions supposedly leading to life. Moreover, it was originally thought that billions of years were available for life to originate by chance. But we now have fossil evidence of life existing as early as 3.8 billion years ago. This means that the "window of opportunity" in which life had to originate by chance is being progressively closed and is now only about 25 million years—which is far too short for the chance scenarios. Moreover, it is essential to chemical origin of life scenarios that the early earth's atmosphere have almost no oxygen; the evidence, however, suggests that the early atmosphere was rich in oxygen. Furthermore, no way existed to preserve any products of chemical evolution for the supposed second step in development. The same processes that formed them serve to destroy them. Thermodynamics also poses an insuperable problem for such scenarios, for there is no way to harness the raw energy of the environment, say, from lightning or the sun, and make it drive chemical evolution forward.

For these reasons and more, the whole field of origin of life studies is in a quandary. All the old theories have broken down; no acceptable new theory is on the horizon. The origin of life on earth seems inexplicable. Francis Crick has mused that the origin of life on earth is "almost a miracle."[28] Because of these problems, a few scientists are saying that maybe life did not originate on earth but was originally carried here by meteorites from some other planet. But that is a leap of pure faith and only pushes the problem back a notch. How did life originate elsewhere? Rather than answer the question, it makes the question unanswerable.

Sometimes people will say that if the universe is infinite in size (or if there are many universes), then no matter how improbable life is, it will originate somewhere by chance. In fact, if the universe is infinite, life will come to exist by chance infinitely many times over throughout the universe. But the problem with this objection is that it multiplies one's probabilistic resources without warrant. If we were allowed to do this, we could explain away virtually any improbable event, so that rational behavior becomes impossible. No matter how improbable something is, we could explain it away by saying that in an infinite universe it would happen somewhere. But can you imagine the following dialogue taking place at a poker table in a west Texas saloon?

"Tex, you're a dirty, cheatin' skunk! Every time you deal you git four aces!"

"Well, Slim, I know it looks a mighty bit suspicious that every time I deals I gits four aces. But you got to understand that in this here infinite universe, there's an infinite number of poker games like this goin' on somewheres. So chances are that in some of 'em, every time I deals, I gits four aces. So put up that shootin' iron and shet yer yap and play cards!"

Now if you were ol' Slim, would you be stupid enough to sit down for another hand of poker? On this kind of reasoning, paradoxically, we could never have any evidence that the universe is infinite, because any evidence for an infinite universe could be explained away as the result of chance in a universe large enough (though still finite) for the evidence to occur by chance alone! Thus, the objection is ultimately self-defeating and cannot be rationally affirmed.

Now the Bible doesn't say how life originated. It just says, "God said, 'Let the land produce vegetation: seed-bearing plants and trees. . . . Let the waters teem with living creatures'" (Genesis 1:11, 20). The Bible is not a science book and doesn't tell us what means, if any, God used to create life. But the scientific evidence is certainly in accord with the origin of life's being, in Francis Crick's words, a miracle, that is, an event that was supernaturally wrought by God. The Bible and science are certainly not in conflict at this point—in fact, if anything, the scientific evidence is clearer than the Bible that life's origin was due to a miraculous act of the Creator God.

HOW LONG ARE THE DAYS OF CREATION IN GENESIS?

Let's pause for a moment to take stock. To begin with, we have the improbability of the initial conditions of the universe being fine-tuned in such a way as to permit life to exist at all in the cosmos. Then on top of that, we must add the improbability of the actual origin of life on the primordial earth. But even with these two conditions in place, there is no guarantee that life would develop into complex organisms. So on top of improbabilities already discussed, we must now add the improbability of the evolution of biological complexity.

This is an issue on which Christians themselves have a variety of viewpoints. Some Christians take Genesis to describe a literal, six-day creation week. But it seems to me that there are clues in the text of Genesis itself that a literal creation week is not intended. For example, the seventh day is clearly not a twenty-four-hour time period but represents God's Sabbath rest from creation that still continues today. We are living in the seventh day. And about the third day, we read, "Then God said, 'Let the land produce vegetation: seed-bearing plants and trees on the land that bear fruit with seed in it, according to their various kinds.' And it was so. The land produced vegetation: plants bearing seed according to their kinds and trees bearing fruit with seed in it according to their kinds. And God saw that it was good. And there was evening, and there was morning—the third day" (Genesis 1:11–13). Now we all know how long it takes for, say, apple trees to grow and blossom and bear fruit. Unless we are to imagine this occurring as in time-lapse photography—like in Walt Disney's movie *The Living Desert*—where plants spring out of the ground and blast into maturity and blossom and fruit pops out, then this must have taken longer than twenty-four hours. I find it hard to believe that the author of Genesis wanted his readers to imagine things popping up like in a film being run on fast-forward. And notice that I'm arguing this on the basis of the text itself, not on the basis of what science tells us.

Historically, neither most Jews nor Christians interpreted Genesis 1 as referring to twenty-four-hour time periods, as the Jewish professor Nathan Aviezer points out in his recent book *In the Beginning.*[29] Aviezer refers to a number of ancient rabbinical scholars on Torah and Talmud to prove the point, and one could also quote early Christian church fathers like Irenaeus, Origen, Basil, and Augustine to show the same thing. I am not denying that a literal reading of Genesis 1 is a legitimate interpretation, but it can hardly claim to be the only interpretation permitted by the text, nor does it represent the historic understanding of the majority of Jews and Christians.

But if this is correct, then Genesis tells us virtually nothing about how God made the plants and animals. Did he create them out of nothing? Did he create them out of existing life-forms? Did he use evolution to produce them gradually? These are scientific questions the Bible does not address. The main point of the Genesis story is to tell us that God is the Creator of everything in the world. The sun and moon and the animals and plants are not deities; they are just creatures: God made them. How he did so seems to be left open.

Now what this means is that the Christian is free to follow the evidence where it leads. In this respect, he or she has a decided advantage over the naturalist. For if God does not exist, then evolution is the only game in town. No matter how improbable the odds, no matter what the evidence says, evolution has to be true, because there is nothing else outside of nature to bring about biological complexity. Thus, the naturalist's conclusion is determined in advance by his or her philosophy, not by the evidence.

Phillip Johnson's book *Darwin on Trial,* which helped to spawn the Intelligent Design movement,[30] shows clearly the central point that the neo-Darwinian theory of evolution is not something that can be read off the evidence but rather is predicated on a philosophical commitment to naturalism. Johnson is quite happy to admit that Darwinism is the best *naturalistic* theory of biological complexity, but since Johnson is not a naturalist, he just says, "So what? What I want to know is not which is the best naturalistic theory, but which theory is *true*." What Johnson argues is that once you drop the presupposition of naturalism, there isn't any compelling evidence that the neo-Darwinian theory is true.

What the evidence supports is microevolution—change within limits. But even the most conservative fundamentalists agree with this, since they believe all human races are descended from a single human ancestral pair, Adam and Eve. So change within certain types is no big deal. The neo-Darwinian theory represents a huge leap or extrapolation from microevolution, which everyone agrees to, to macroevolution. But examples are common in science where such extrapolations fail. For example, Einstein tried to extrapolate from his successful special principle of relativity to a general principle of relativity. But he proved unable to do so. The general theory of relativity is really a misnomer, since it is actually a theory of gravity and does not succeed in making all motion relative, as Einstein had hoped. In the same way, we must ask, why think that the extrapolation of microevolution to macroevolution is legitimate? Once we drop a methodological commitment to naturalism, why think that the neo-Darwinian theory is true?

IS THE NEO-DARWINIAN THEORY OF EVOLUTION TRUE?

The question of whether the neo-Darwinian theory of biological evolution is true is much subtler than most people realize. Part of the problem lies in the ambiguity of the word *evolution,* which is sometimes taken to mean no more than "change over time," which nobody disagrees with. We therefore need to move beyond the terminology and look at what the theory actually holds. There are at least two main tenets of the neo-Darwinian theory of biological evolution: first, what we may call the doctrine of common ancestry, and second, the mechanisms of genetic mutation and natural selection.

According to the doctrine of common ancestry, all life-forms evolved from a single primordial ancestor. In favor of this doctrine is the fact that almost all living organisms share the same genetic code, or DNA. One could say that God simply used the same basic design plan to make the different kinds of separate organisms he made. But it might seem more plausible that the genetic similarity of all living things is due to their being related to each other, all sharing a common ancestor.

On the other hand, the fossil evidence stands starkly in opposition to the doctrine of common ancestry. When Darwin proposed his theory, one of its major weaknesses was that no organisms stood midway between other organisms as transitional forms. Darwin answered this, however, by saying that these transitional animals existed in the past and would eventually be discovered. But as paleontologists have unearthed fossil remains, they have not found these transitional forms; they have just found more distinct animals and plants that have died off. Sure, there are a few suspected transitional forms, like the Archaeopteryx, a bird with some reptilian features. But if neo-Darwinian theory were true, there would not be only a few, rare missing links; rather, as Michael Denton emphasizes, there would be literally millions of transitional forms in the fossil record.[31] Think, for example, of all the intermediate forms that would have to exist for a bat and a whale to have evolved from a common ancestor! The problem can no longer be dismissed by saying that we haven't dug deep enough. The transitional forms haven't been found because they aren't there. Thus, the evidence concerning the doctrine of common ancestry is mixed. The DNA evidence lends some support to it, but the fossil evidence goes against it.

What about the mechanisms of genetic mutation and natural selection, which are supposed to drive evolution? According to the theory, evolutionary development occurs because random mutations produce new features in living things, and those that are advantageous for survival are preserved and get reproduced.

I know of no evidence at all that these mechanisms are capable of producing the sort of biological complexity we see in the world today from an original single-celled organism. In fact, the evidence is positively against it. For one thing, the processes are just too slow. In their book *The Anthropic Cosmological Principle,* Barrow and Tipler list ten steps in the course of human evolution—the development of aerobic respiration, the development of an inner skeleton, the development of the eye, for example—each of which is so improbable that before it would occur, the sun would have ceased to be a main sequence star and incinerated the earth![32] They conclude, "There has developed a general consensus among evolutionists that the evolution of intelligent life is so improbable that it is unlikely to have occurred on any other planet in the entire visible universe."[33] If this is true, why think that intelligent life evolved by chance on *this* planet?

A second problem with genetic mutation and natural selection is that they cannot explain the origin of irreducibly complex systems. This is the main point of Michael Behe's book *Darwin's Black Box.*[34] Behe, who is a microbiologist at Lehigh University, points out that certain systems in the cell, like the blood-clotting mechanisms or the hairlike structures called cilia, are like incredibly complicated, microscopic machines that cannot function at all unless all the parts are present and functioning. Thus, they cannot evolve piecemeal. Surveying thousands of scientific articles on these systems, Behe discovered that virtually nothing has ever been written on how such irreducibly complex systems could have evolved by random mutation and natural selection.[35] There is no scientific understanding whatsoever about how such systems originated; with respect to them, Darwinism has absolutely no explanatory power.

In sum, in the absence of a methodological commitment to naturalism, there really does not appear to be compelling evidence for the neo-Darwinian theory. On the contrary, there seems to be pretty persuasive evidence that the neo-Darwinian account cannot be the full story. Again, the Bible does not tell us how God created biologically complex organisms any more than it tells us how he created life. (The account of the creation of man and woman in Genesis 2 is obviously highly symbolic, since God, not having lungs or a mouth, didn't literally blow into Adam's nose.) He could have created *ex nihilo* (out of nothing), or he could have used lower stages of living organisms as raw material for the creation of higher forms through systemic changes that would have been wholly improbable on any naturalistic account. The Christian is open to follow the evidence where it leads. But what the evidence does seem to indicate is that the existence of biological complexity demands a designing intelligence such as the Bible describes.

Conclusion

The above is just an inadequate sample of the exciting and interesting work being done today in the science and religion dialogue. Much, much more deserves to be said—for example, about quantum theory and relativity theory, anthropology and neurology. Difficult questions remain; but the contemporary evangelical should not fear science as an enemy of Christian faith. Rather, he or she should embrace science as an ally in understanding the truth about the world God has created and as a rich apologetic resource for commending Christian faith.

QUESTIONS FOR REFLECTION AND DISCUSSION

1. How would you respond to someone who says that because science answers the "What?" questions and religion answers the "Why?" questions, they therefore can never come into conflict?

2. If someone were to ask you, "What scientific evidence is there for God?" what would you say?

3. Suppose a Christian high school student, perhaps your daughter or son, came to you saying that they think God may be calling her or him into a career as a professional scientist. What would be your reaction, and what advice would you give?

Chapter 4

TOUGH QUESTIONS ABOUT CHRIST

LEE STROBEL

As the new millennium dawned, ABC news anchor Peter Jennings caused a national furor when he aired a controversial television special purporting to be a "search for Jesus." He set the bar low at the outset by declaring, "We cannot tell you whether Jesus is the Son of God; that is a matter of faith." Then he proceeded to present the dogmatic assertions of left-wing theologians that the Bible is hopelessly riddled with contradictions, that Mary was probably impregnated by a Roman soldier, that Jesus wasn't really born in Bethlehem, that his healings were undoubtedly psychosomatic, and that he didn't rise from the dead. It was a stunning display of uncritical and lopsided reporting that quite justifiably led to widespread criticism.

In an early scene, Jennings speculated about whether a certain rock uncovered by archaeologists could actually be a place where the pregnant Mary rested during her journey. With evidence for this possibility being admittedly sparse, he added, "Right here we realized just how difficult it would be for a journalist to get the story right." The clear implication was that any evidence for the much more significant aspects of Jesus' life, such as his resurrection, would be equally speculative.

I was extremely disappointed by Jennings's report, particularly because I had conducted my own two-year investigation into the evidence for Jesus. Like Jennings, I was a journalist. Trained at the University of Missouri's journalism school and Yale Law School, I was the legal affairs editor for *The Chicago Tribune* and an adamant atheist. In 1980 my wife's conversion to Christianity prompted me to launch a personal inquiry into whether there was any credibility to the faith. Unlike Jennings, however, I thoroughly checked out a wide range of scholarly assessments of Jesus. I sought to dig beneath the surface of mere opinion and down to the bedrock of historical fact. The result: My conclusions were far different from his.

While Jennings imagined a gaping gulf between the Jesus of history and the Christ of faith, I became convinced—mostly against my hopes at the time—that they are actually one and the same. Indeed, the evidence for the resurrection of Jesus proved so overwhelming to me that I felt I had no choice but to accept it as the ultimate authentication of Jesus' claim of deity. Compelled by the facts of history, I repented of my sin and received Christ as my forgiver and leader on November 8, 1981. What I thought would be the end of a journey turned out to be the beginning of a breathtaking adventure as a follower of Jesus.[1]

Today my ministry takes me around the world and into encounters with all kinds of cynics, skeptics, and seekers. Many of them are mired in misinformation about Jesus, partially because of the efforts of members of the radical Jesus Seminar to mainstream their skeptical conclusions into a public marketplace where people are ill-equipped to appropriately evaluate them.

Unaware that the liberal Jesus Seminar is composed of only a tiny minority of New Testament scholars and is a hotbed of poorly substantiated speculations, more and more members of the public find themselves influenced by its approach. They conclude that the Jesus Seminar (which votes on the authenticity of Jesus' statements and denies his miracles) and like-minded academics represent "real" scholarship that deals in indisputable facts, while they dismiss those who take a more conservative approach as being mere propagandists who are pushing the wishful thinking of faith.[2]

The pivotal question that Jesus posed to his disciples—"Who do you say I am?" (Matthew 16:15)—continues to reverberate through history, challenging each individual to decide whether he was a mere man, as Jennings's report seemed to suggest, or the unique Son of God, as orthodox Christianity has affirmed through the centuries. Rather than swallow the Enlightenment's phony distinction between the Jesus of faith and the Jesus of facts, I concluded that it is the very facts of history that point powerfully toward the reasonableness of faith in the deity of Christ.[3]

As I have sought to articulate the case for Jesus in my personal encounters with skeptics and in my preaching at church services designed to reach spiritual seekers, I find myself consistently dealing with five strands of evidence that weave a cogent and convincing apologetic for Christ. Each one of them answers a specific question that is either on the lips or lurking in the back of the minds of people who are investigating whether Christianity can withstand intellectual scrutiny. They begin with the foundational issue of whether the documents that purport to record the life of Jesus can be trusted.

ARE THE RECORDS OF JESUS' LIFE RELIABLE?

In his television special, Jennings was quick to accept the skepticism of liberal professors toward Matthew, Mark, Luke, and John, the Gospels that describe the life, teachings, miracles, death, and resurrection of Jesus. "Scholars told us early on that they don't take everything they read in the New Testament literally, because the New Testament has four different and sometimes contradictory versions of Jesus' life," he said. "There is no reliable evidence about who the authors actually were. It is pretty much agreed that they were not eyewitnesses. In fact, the Gospels were probably written 40 to 100 years after Jesus' death."

Skeptics must try to dismantle the reliability of the Gospels in order to undermine their clear teaching that Jesus is the one and only Son of God. However, there is excellent scholarship that supports the fundamental accuracy and reliability of the Gospel accounts. As Peter Stuhlmacher, professor emeritus at the Protestant Theological Faculty in Tübingen, told *Time* magazine for an article on the identity of Jesus, "The biblical texts as they stand are the best hypothesis we have until now to explain what really happened."[4]

Craig Blomberg, professor of New Testament at Denver Seminary and author of *The Historical Reliability of the Gospels,* conceded that, strictly speaking, the Gospels are anonymous. Nevertheless, he stressed that the uniform testimony of the early church was that Matthew, the tax collector and one of the twelve disciples, was the author of the first Gospel in the New Testament; John Mark, a companion of the disciple Peter, wrote the Gospel we call Mark; and Luke, known as Paul's "beloved physician," wrote the Gospel of Luke and the Acts of the Apostles.

While the name of the author of the fourth Gospel isn't in doubt—it is certainly John—there was a question concerning whether this was John the apostle or a different John. Blomberg, though, said he is convinced that "a substantial majority of the material goes back to the apostle," although someone closely associated with John may have acted as an editor, "putting the last verses into shape and potentially creating the stylistic uniformity of the entire document." In any event, he emphasized, "the Gospel is obviously based on eyewitness material, as are the other three Gospels."[5]

The authorship of Mark and Matthew was affirmed by Papias in A.D. 125. Then Irenaeus confirmed this in A.D. 180:

> Matthew published his own Gospel among the Hebrews in their own tongue, when Peter and Paul were preaching the Gospel in Rome and founding the church there. After their departure, Mark, the disciple and interpreter of Peter, himself handed down to us in writing the substance of Peter's preaching. Luke, the follower of Paul, set down in a book the Gospel preached by his teacher. Then John, the disciple of the Lord, who also leaned on his breast, himself produced his Gospel while he was living at Ephesus in Asia.[6]

Significantly, observed Blomberg, there is no evidence from the first century that the authorship of the Gospels was ever in doubt. In fact, if authorship was going to be invented, certainly names of prominent apostles such as Peter or James would have been used in an attempt to bolster credibility rather than to attribute the Gospels to Mark and Luke, who weren't even among the twelve disciples, and Matthew, who was formerly a hated tax collector.

The Complementary Gospels

The frequently asserted allegation that the Gospels contradict each other has been exhaustively dealt with in a variety of books. "In reality, far from being contradictory, the Gospels are clearly complementary," said Hank Hanegraaff of the Christian Research Institute. "Throughout the centuries, countless Bible scholars and commentaries have attested to that fact. Had all the Gospel writers said the exact same thing in the exact same way, they could have legitimately been questioned on the grounds of collusion."[7]

Apologist Norman Geisler, president of Southern Evangelical Seminary, has collected about eight hundred alleged biblical contradictions. "All I can tell you is that in my experience, when critics raise these objections, they invariably violate one of seventeen principles for interpreting Scripture," he told me in an interview.

As an example, just because the Gospels take a different perspective in describing events doesn't mean they are irreconcilable. Matthew says there was one angel at Jesus' tomb, while John says there were two, yet Geisler points out that "Matthew didn't say there was *only* one. John was providing more detail by saying there were two."[8]

After studying the consistency among the four Gospels, Simon Greenleaf of Harvard Law School, the nineteenth-century's greatest expert on legal evidence, concluded: "There is enough of a discrepancy to show that there could have been no previous concert among them and at the same time such substantial agreement as to show that they all were independent narrators of the same great transaction."[9]

The Evidence of Archaeology

Archaeology also has corroborated the essential reliability of the New Testament. Time after time, when incidental details of the New Testament can be checked out, they emerge as being accurate. For instance, John 5:1–15 describes how Jesus healed an invalid by the pool at Bethesda, which John describes as having five porticoes. Archaeologist John McRay said skeptics have long cited this as an example of John being inaccurate, because no such place had been found—until more recently when the pool was excavated and scientists discovered five porticoes or colonnaded porches, just as John had described.[10]

Luke, who wrote one-quarter of the New Testament, has been found to be a scrupulously accurate historian, even in the smallest details. One archaeologist carefully studied Luke's references to thirty-two countries, fifty-four cities, and nine islands, finding not a single error.[11] "The general consensus of both liberal and conservative scholars is that Luke is very accurate as a historian," said McRay.[12]

All of this leads to this important question: If the New Testament writers were so careful to be exceedingly accurate in even the most minor and incidental details, wouldn't they have been equally or even more careful in reporting on truly significant events, such as the miracles, teachings, death, and resurrection of Jesus?

"Those who know the facts," concluded Australian archaeologist Clifford Wilson, "now recognize that the New Testament must be accepted as a remarkably accurate source book."[13]

The Early Dating of the Gospels

Another way critics attempt to discredit the Gospels is to hypothesize that they were written so long after the events that legend, mythology, and wishful thinking crept in and thoroughly corrupted the accounts. Indeed, those with an antisupernatural bias are forced to date the Gospels after the fall of Jerusalem in A.D. 70, because they don't believe Jesus could have predicted this event as he is recorded as doing in Matthew 24, Mark 13, and Luke 21. Even Peter Jennings sought to date the Gospels from forty to one hundred years after the life of Jesus. However, there are solid reasons for concluding that the Gospels actually were written much closer to Jesus' death (which probably occurred in A.D. 33) and that legendary development could not have rendered them unreliable.

Craig Blomberg pointed out that even standard liberal dating of the Gospels—Mark in the A.D. 70s, Matthew and Luke in the 80s, and John in the 90s—is "still within the lifetimes of various eyewitnesses of the life of Jesus, including hostile eyewitnesses who would have served as a corrective if false teachings about Jesus were going around."[14]

However, Blomberg and many other New Testament experts believe there are solid reasons for dating the Gospels even earlier than this. Prominent apologist J. P. Moreland, a professor at the Talbot School of Theology, articulates several reasons that form a powerful case for Acts having been written between A.D. 62 and 64. For example, Acts doesn't mention several monumental events that it surely would have included if it had been written after they occurred. These include the fall of Jerusalem in A.D. 70; Nero's persecutions in the mid 60s; the martyrdoms of James (61), Paul (64), and Peter (65); and the Jewish war against the Romans from 66 onward. Also, many of the expressions in Acts are very early and primitive, and the book deals with issues that were especially important prior to Jerusalem's fall.[15]

Because Acts is the second of a two-part work authored by Luke, this means his Gospel must have been written before the early A.D. 60s, or within thirty years of Jesus' life. Since Luke drew some of his information from the Gospel of Mark, it makes sense that Mark must come even earlier than this. Moreland concluded, "The picture of Jesus presented in the Synoptics [Matthew, Mark, and Luke] is one that is only twelve to twenty-nine years removed from the events themselves. And they incorporate sources which are even earlier."[16]

What's more, the New Testament also features letters by the apostle Paul that are dated as early as A.D. 49. His high Christology—that Jesus is God and the Lord of heaven and earth—does not evolve through his various writings and thus "must have been largely completed before he began his great missionary journeys ... that is, by 48," Moreland said.[17] And, he added, Paul includes some creeds and hymns that predate his own writings and that "present a portrait of a miraculous and divine Jesus who rose from the dead."[18]

Moreland concluded, "In sum, the idea of a fully divine, miracle-working Jesus who rose from the dead was present during the first decade of Christianity. Such a view was not a legend which arose several decades after the crucifixion." Indeed, he said, Paul's writings in Galatians, where he describes meeting with the apostles in Jerusalem and confirming that his message of Christ's deity was correct, coupled with an extremely early creed about the resurrection found in 1 Corinthians 15, demonstrate that "belief in a divine, risen Jesus was in existence within just a few years after his death."[19]

This takes on added significance in light of a study by A. N. Sherwin-White, respected Greco-Roman classical historian from Oxford University, which established that the passage of two generations was not even enough time for legend to develop in the ancient world and wipe out a solid core of historical truth.[20] In the case of Jesus, we have reliable information about his divinity and resurrection that falls safely within that span.

Passing the Manuscript Test

In addition, the wealth of manuscript evidence for the New Testament gives us confidence that these writings have been transmitted to us through history in an accurate way. Archaeologists have uncovered more than five thousand ancient New Testament Greek manuscripts, with fragments dating back as early as the second century. Counting Latin Vulgate manuscripts and others, the total is twenty-four thousand manuscripts in existence. Next to the New Testament, the greatest manuscript evidence for any other ancient work is for Homer's *Iliad,* of which there are fewer than 650 manuscripts that come a full thousand years after the original writing.

"In no other case is the interval of time between the composition of the book and the date of the earliest manuscripts so short as in that of the New Testament," said Sir Frederic Kenyon, former director of the British Museum and author of *The Palaeography of Greek Papyri.*[21] "The last foundation for any doubt that the scriptures have come down to us substantially as they were written has now been removed."[22]

Because of the foundational importance of the New Testament, my analysis of its reliability consumed much of my two-year investigation into

Christianity when I was a skeptic. I subjected the Gospels to eight tests they might face in a court of law—the intention test, the ability test, the character test, the consistency test, the bias test, the cover-up test, the corroboration test, and the adverse witness test—to determine whether they could be considered trustworthy.[23] My verdict was that their essential reliability is beyond serious doubt.

DID JESUS EVER CLAIM TO BE GOD?

I hear the objection all the time: Jesus never really claimed he was the Son of God; instead, this belief was superimposed on the Jesus tradition by overzealous followers years after his death. The real Jesus saw himself as nothing more than a rabbi, a sage, an iconoclastic rabble-rouser—anything but God. Or, at least, this is what critics claim. But it is not what the evidence clearly shows. The truth was summarized by Scottish theologian H. R. Macintosh: "The self-consciousness of Jesus . . . is the greatest fact in history."[24]

Kevin Vanhoozer, research professor of systematic theology at Trinity Evangelical Divinity School, put the issue this way: "Jesus understood himself to be the beloved Son of God, chosen by God to bring about the kingdom of God and the forgiveness of sins. Our understanding of who Jesus was must correspond to Jesus' own self-understanding. If we do not confess Jesus as the Christ, then either he was deluded about his identity or we are."[25]

At least ten factors point toward Jesus as believing he was the one and only Son of God. First, there was the way he referred to himself. No scholar doubts that the most common way Jesus referred to himself was "the Son of Man," which he applied to himself more than four dozen times, including in Mark, generally considered the earliest gospel. While some critics mistakenly believe this is a mere claim of humanity, the scholarly consensus is that this is a reference to Daniel 7:13–14, where the Son of Man is ushered into the very presence of the Almighty, has "authority, glory and sovereign power," receives the worship of "all peoples," and is someone whose dominion is everlasting.

"The Son of Man was a divine figure in the Old Testament book of Daniel who would come at the end of the world to judge mankind and rule forever," said theologian and philosopher William Lane Craig. "Thus, the claim to be the Son of Man would be in effect a claim to divinity."[26]

Vanhoozer adds an interesting sidelight: "The curious thing about Jesus' use of the title . . . is that he linked it not only with the theme of future glory but also with the theme of suffering and death. In doing so, Jesus was teaching his disciples something new about the long-awaited Messiah, namely, that his suffering would precede his glory (e.g., Luke 9:22)."[27]

Second, Vanhoozer points out that Jesus also made a claim of divinity when he applied the "I am" sayings to himself, at one point declaring, "I tell you the truth, before Abraham was born, I am!" (John 8:58). This obvious allusion to God's words to Moses out of the burning bush was such an unmistakable declaration of equality with God that his audience picked up stones to hurl at him for blasphemy.[28]

Third, Jesus made a divine claim when he forgave the sins of the paralytic in Mark 2. "The only person who can say that sort of thing meaningfully is God himself, because sin, even if it is against other people, is first and foremost a defiance of God and his laws," observed theologian D. A. Carson.[29]

Fourth, there was even a transcendent claim made by the way Jesus selected his disciples, according to Ben Witherington III, author of *The Christology of Jesus.* "If the Twelve represent a renewed Israel, where does Jesus fit in?" he asked. "He's not just part of Israel, not merely part of the redeemed group, he's forming the group—just as God in the Old Testament formed his people and set up the twelve tribes of Israel. That's a clue about what Jesus thought of himself."[30]

A fifth clue about Jesus' self-understanding comes through the way he taught. "[Jesus] begins his teachings with the phrase 'Amen I say to you,' which is to say, 'I swear in advance to the truthfulness of what I'm about to say.' This was absolutely revolutionary," Witherington said. He went on to explain:

In Judaism, you needed the testimony of two witnesses ... but Jesus witnesses to the truth of his own sayings. Instead of basing his teaching on the authority of others, he speaks on his own authority.

So here is someone who considered himself to have authority above and beyond what the Old Testament prophets had. He believed he possessed not only divine inspiration, as King David did, but also divine authority and the power of direct divine utterance.[31]

Sixth, Jesus used the Aramaic term *Abba,* or "Father dearest," when relating to God. This reflects an intimacy that was alien in ancient Judaism, in which devout Jews avoided the use of God's personal name out of fear they may mispronounce it. Dr. Witherington made this observation:

> The significance of "Abba" is that Jesus is the initiator of an intimate relationship that was previously unavailable. The question is, What kind of person can initiate a new covenantal relationship with God? ...
>
> Jesus is saying that only through having a relationship with him does this kind of prayer language—this kind of "Abba" relationship with God—become possible. That says volumes about how he regarded himself.[32]

A seventh indicator of Jesus' self-understanding can be seen in his postresurrection encounter with the apostle Thomas in John 20. Responding to Jesus' invitation to personally check out the evidence that he had really risen from the dead, Thomas declares in verse 28, "My Lord and my God!" Jesus' reply was telling. It would have been the height of blasphemy for him to have knowingly received Thomas's worship unless Jesus really was God. Yet instead of rebuking him, Jesus said in verse 29, "Because you have seen me, you have believed; blessed are those who have not seen and yet have believed." Jesus' choice to receive Thomas's worship clearly means he believed he was God and thus worthy of that homage. Similarly, when Simon Peter answered Jesus' question, "Who do you say I am?" by saying, "You are the Christ, the Son of the living God," Jesus' reaction was not to correct him but rather to affirm that this was revealed to him by the Father himself (see Matthew 16:15–17).

Eighth, Jesus clearly believed that the eternal destiny of people hinged on whether they believed in him. "If you do not believe I am the one I claim to be," he said in John 8:24, "you will indeed die in your sins." In addition, he said in Luke 12:8–9: "I tell you, whoever acknowledges me before men, the Son of Man will also acknowledge him before the angels of God. But he who disowns me before men will be disowned before the angels of God." William Lane Craig put the implication this way: "Make no mistake: if Jesus were not the divine Son of God, then this claim could only be regarded as the most narrow and objectionable dogmatism. For Jesus is saying that people's salvation depends on their confession to Jesus himself."[33]

An equally overt assertion of divinity is found in John 10:30, where Jesus declared outright, "I and the Father are one." There is no question about whether his listeners understood that Jesus was saying that he and God are one in substance. Promptly, they picked up rocks to attack him "for blasphemy, because you, a mere man, claim to be God" (verse 33).

A tenth factor that should be weighed in assessing Jesus' belief about his identity is his miracles, which will be discussed in the next section. Jesus stressed that his feats were a sign of the coming of God's kingdom: "If I drive out demons by the finger of God, then the kingdom of God has come to you" (Luke 11:20). Ben Witherington observed that even though others in the Bible also performed miracles, this statement showed that Jesus didn't merely regard himself as a wonder-worker: "He sees himself as the one in whom and through whom the promises of God come to pass. And that's a not-too-thinly-veiled claim of transcendence."[34]

Said British scholar James D. G. Dunn, "Whatever the 'facts' were, Jesus evidently believed that he had cured cases of blindness, lameness, and deafness—indeed, there is no reason to doubt that he believed lepers had been cured under his ministry and dead restored to life."[35]

Fulfilling the Attributes of God

Of course, anyone can believe that he or she is God. Jesus didn't just consider himself God's Son, but he also fulfilled the attributes that are unique to God. Philippians 2 describes how Jesus emptied himself of the independent use of his attributes—a phenomenon termed *kenosis*—when he was incarnated. This explains how he didn't always choose to exhibit the "omnis"—omniscience, omnipotence, and omnipresence—in his earthly existence. Even so, the New Testament confirms that all of these qualities were ultimately true of him. For example, in John 16:30, John affirms of Jesus, "Now we can see that you know all things," which is omniscience. In Matthew 28:20, Jesus is recorded as saying, "Surely I am with you always, to the very end of the age," which is omnipresence. And he declared, "All authority in heaven and on earth has been given to me" (Matthew 28:18), which is omnipotence.

Indeed, Colossians 2:9 reads, "For in Christ all the fullness of the Deity lives in bodily form." His eternality is confirmed in John 1:1, which declares of Jesus, "In the beginning was the Word, and the Word was with God, and the Word was God." His immutability is shown in Hebrews 13:8: "Jesus Christ is the same yesterday and today and forever." His sinlessness is seen in John 8:29: "The one who sent me is with me; he has not left me alone, for I always do what pleases him." Hebrews 1:3 declares Jesus to be "the radiance of God's glory and the exact representation of his being." Colossians 1:17 says, "In him all things hold together." Matthew 25:31–32 affirms he will be the judge of humankind. And in Hebrews 1:8, the Father himself specifically makes reference to Jesus as being God.

In fact, the very names used to paint a portrait of God in the Old Testament—names such as Alpha and Omega, Lord, Savior, King, Judge, Light, Rock, Redeemer, Shepherd, Creator, giver of life, forgiver of sin, and speaker with divine authority—also are applied to Jesus in the New Testament.

Who did Jesus believe he was? In his book *New Approaches to Jesus and the Gospels,* Royce Gruenler, professor of New Testament at Gordon-Conwell Theological Seminary, comes to this conclusion: "It is a striking fact of modern New Testament research that the essential clues for correctly reading the implicit christological self-understanding of Jesus are abundantly clear."[36]

Beyond just believing he was God, though, Jesus also proved it by working supernatural deeds, by fulfilling ancient prophecies against all mathematical odds, and ultimately by conquering the grave—the three very important topics considered in the next chapter.

QUESTIONS FOR REFLECTION AND DISCUSSION

1. Jesus asked his disciples, "Who do you say I am?" How would you answer this question? What evidence would you use to support your conclusion?

2. What evidence for the reliability of the Gospels is most compelling to you? Why?

3. If Jesus believed he was God and fulfilled the attributes of God, then what are three implications, first, for other religions and, second, for yourself?

Chapter 5

MORE TOUGH QUESTIONS ABOUT CHRIST

LEE STROBEL

As British pastor John Stott has pointed out, Jesus clearly asserted that "to know him was to know God; to see him was to see God; to believe in him was to believe in God; to receive him was to receive God; to hate him was to hate God; and to honor him was to honor God."[1] But the critical question is this: How do we know Jesus was telling the truth?

As a journalist at *The Chicago Tribune,* I had encountered plenty of bizarre people who claimed they were God, but this didn't prompt me to bend down and worship them. I needed more than merely a bald assertion; I needed evidence. And the same was true in my spiritual investigation of Jesus. He may have claimed to be the unique Son of God, but did he do anything to back up this contention?

This issue leads me to three more tough questions often raised about Jesus. These topics focus on whether he was able to perform miracles, fulfill the ancient messianic prophecies, and return from the dead—achievements which, if true, provide compelling confirmation of his claim to being God's unique Son.

DID JESUS REALLY PERFORM MIRACLES?

In the twenty-first century, when scientists have mapped the human genome, dissected the atom, and peered through the Hubble telescope into the distant reaches of the universe, many people believe the rationality of science should chase away naive belief in the supernatural.

The late agnostic astronomer Carl Sagan taught, "The Cosmos is all that is or ever was or ever will be."[2] Evangelist-turned-agnostic Charles Templeton insisted that "it is time to be done with primitive speculation and superstition and look at life in rational terms."[3] Atheistic evolutionist Richard Dawkins mocked the miracles of the Old and New Testaments by saying that "they are very effective with an audience of unsophisticates and children."[4] Liberal professor John Dominic Crossan scoffed, "I do not think that anyone, anywhere, at any time brings dead people back to life."[5]

Putting faith in the concrete "facts" of science over the supernatural of Scripture, the Jesus Seminar's book *The Five Gospels* declares flatly, "The Christ of creed and dogma, who had been firmly in place in the Middle Ages, can no longer command the assent of those who have seen the heavens through Galileo's telescope. The old deities and demons were swept from the skies by that remarkable glass."[6]

These opinions are squarely at odds with the Bible's claim that God has performed miracles throughout history. In fact, Genesis insists that all of history began with the astounding miracle of God creating everything out of nothing. In the case of Jesus, miracles are important in confirming his divine identity. He actually boldly declared, "Do not believe me unless I do what my Father does [namely, miracles]" (John 10:37). The prophet Isaiah indicated that miracles would be one way the Messiah would authenticate himself (see Isaiah 35:5–6). And the New Testament says Jesus did perform supernatural feats by healing the sick, turning water into wine, multiplying the fish and loaves, walking on the sea, and even raising the dead.

It is important to set the groundwork by observing that if God exists, we should have no problem believing he has the ability to intervene in his creation in a miraculous way. For a long time, Christians have used the cosmological argument, the teleological argument, the ontological argument, the argument from moral law, the argument from religious need, and other reasoning and evidence to persuasively build the case that God does exist.[7]

"The only way to show that miracles are impossible," observed Norman Geisler, "is to disprove the existence of God."[8] And nobody has ever been able to do that.

The evidence that Jesus authenticated his claim to being God by performing miracles can be demonstrated through six points.

1. The Reliability of the New Testament

We saw in the preceding chapter that the Gospels that describe Jesus' miracles can be traced back to eyewitness material, have been confirmed by archaeology where they can be checked out, and have been passed down through the centuries with fidelity. In addition, historian Gary Habermas, author of *The Historical Jesus,* has detailed thirty-nine ancient sources outside the Bible that provide further corroboration for more than one hundred facts about Jesus' life, teachings, death, and resurrection.[9]

In light of the antisupernatural presuppositions of the Jesus Seminar and others, British New Testament scholar R. T. France's assessment of the Gospels is particularly relevant:

> At the level of their literary and historical character we have good reasons to treat the gospels seriously as a source of information on the life and teaching of Jesus, and thus on the historical origins of Christianity. . . . Beyond that point the decision as to how far a scholar is willing to accept the record they offer is likely to be influenced more by his openness to a "supernaturalist" worldview than by strictly historical considerations.[10]

Miracles are found in all strata of the Gospels. For example, many scholars hypothesize that an ancient source of Jesus' sayings, which they call "Q," was used as a source by Matthew and Luke. Thus, it would contain very primitive information whose essential trustworthiness would not have been ruined by legendary development. "Even in Q, there is clearly an awareness of Jesus' ministry of miracles," Craig Blomberg, author of *The Historical Reliability of the Gospels,* observes.[11] For example, when John the Baptist's disciples asked Jesus if he really was the Christ, he essentially told them to consider his miracles of healing and raising the dead as evidence (see Matthew 11:2–6; Luke 7:18–23).

In addition, the miracle of the feeding of the five thousand is found in all the Gospels, "so you have independent, multiple attestation to these events," said William Lane Craig, research professor of philosophy at Talbot School of Theology. He stressed, "There is no vestige of a non-miraculous Jesus of Nazareth in any of the sources."[12] This is even true of the four independent sources that the skeptical Jesus Seminar recognizes behind Matthew, Mark, and Luke.[13]

Consequently, most New Testament critics—including some of the most skeptical—have been forced to concede that Jesus did perform miracles. "Granted, they may not all believe these were *genuine* miracles," William Lane Craig observes, "but the idea of Jesus of Nazareth as a miracle-worker and exorcist is part of the historical Jesus that's generally accepted by critics today."[14]

2. The Inclusion of Historical Details Lends Credibility

Scholars have noted that some miracle accounts have historical elements in incidental details that give credence to the reports. For example, specifically listing Lazarus as the name of the person raised from the dead would allow first-century skeptics to investigate the matter for themselves. Also, the Gospel accounts are sober and simple, almost journalistic in style, unlike the fanciful supernatural occurrences described in later apocryphal gospels.[15]

Scholar Stephen Davis pointed out that in the story of Jesus turning water into wine, material is included that would be counterproductive to Jesus. For example, the apparently harsh way he spoke to his mother is difficult to explain. Even reporting the story at all could fuel charges that Jesus was a glutton and drunkard, as some alleged (see Matthew 11:19). Thus, it would be unlikely that the church would later invent such a story.[16]

3. Jewish Leaders and Jesus' Opponents Admitted He Performed Miracles

In John 3 a Pharisee named Nicodemus, a member of the Jewish ruling council, said to Jesus, "Rabbi, we know you are a teacher who has come from God. For no one could perform the miraculous signs you are doing if God were not with him" (John 3:2). This is confirmation from outside Jesus' followers that he was known for doing miracles. Paul records in 1 Corinthians 15:7–8 the fact that both he, who had been a persecutor of Christians, and James, who had been a skeptic of Jesus, encountered the miraculously resurrected Jesus and became convinced of his divinity as a result.

4. Antagonistic Sources outside the Bible Confirm Jesus' Miracles

Ancient Jewish writings known as the Talmud contain some derisive comments about Jesus. However, they also confirm several historical facts about him, including that he dealt in the supernatural (although the Talmud seeks to denigrate Jesus by attributing his power to "sorcery").[17]

Also, Norman Geisler has pointed out that Muhammad believed Jesus to have been a prophet who performed miracles, including raising the dead. Geisler adds, "That's very interesting, because in the Koran when unbelievers challenged Muhammad to perform a miracle, he refused. He merely said they should read a chapter in the Koran."[18]

There is even some indication that Jesus' own executioner may have borne witness to his supernatural abilities. Christian apologist Justin Martyr reported around A.D. 150 that the Acts of Pilate, an official document that had purportedly been sent to Rome, attested to the crucifixion as well as several healing miracles that Jesus had performed.[19] Though the apologetic value of Justin's assertions is minimal today because the authentic report from Pilate, if it ever existed, is no longer available, it is fascinating to note that Justin encouraged his readers to check out the Acts of Pilate for themselves to confirm what he was saying. Why would he do that unless he was absolutely confident that Pilate's writings would back him up?[20]

5. The Miraculous Resurrection Is One of the Best-Attested Events in the Ancient World

Jesus' climactic miracle was his return from the dead after his brutal execution at the hands of the Romans. As the last section of this chapter describes, there is compelling historical evidence to conclude that Jesus' resurrection is an actual event.

6. Alternative Explanations Fall Short

Some critics have tried to postulate theories to explain away Jesus' miracles, but all of them crumble under scrutiny. For example, Charles Templeton proposed that Jesus' healings could have been merely psychosomatic.[21] Although Gary Collins, a university professor of psychology for more than twenty years, said he couldn't rule out that Jesus might have sometimes healed by suggestion, it certainly cannot account for all of his miracles. In an interview, he made this observation:

> Often a psychosomatic healing takes time; Jesus' healings were spontaneous. Many times people who are healed psychologically have their symptoms return a few days later, but we don't see any evidence of this. And Jesus healed conditions like lifelong blindness and leprosy, for which a psychosomatic explanation isn't very likely. On top of that, he brought people back from the dead—and death is not a psychologically induced state! Plus you have all of his nature miracles—the calming of the sea, turning water into wine. They defy naturalistic answers.[22]

Collins is right. Naturalistic explanations fail to account for the range, type, and circumstances of Jesus' miracles. In addition, allegations that Jesus' miracles were myths inspired by prior stories of Hellenistic divine men or ancient Jewish holy men cannot withstand scrutiny. After studying the differences and similarities between those stories and the Gospels, Gary Habermas said, "It cannot be proven that ancient parallels account for the Gospel reports."[23]

My conclusion is that the historical accounts of Jesus' supernatural works of healing, exorcism, and power over nature are authentic and that they are additional confirmation of his identity as the Son of God. "The cumulative case," as Habermas notes, "shows that the Gospels are correct in reporting that Jesus performed miracles."[24]

DID JESUS FULFILL THE MESSIANIC PROPHECIES?

In an interview, Norman Geisler, from his vast collection of quotes from skeptics, told me about the response of agnostic Bertrand Russell when he was asked what it would take for him to believe in God:

I think that if I heard a voice from the sky predicting all that was going to happen to me during the next twenty-four hours, including events that would have seemed highly improbable, and if all these events then proceed to happen, then I might perhaps be convinced at least of the existence of some superhuman intelligence. I can imagine other evidence of the same sort which might convince me, but as far as I know, no such evidence exists.[25]

Asked how he would reply to Russell, Geisler smiled and said, "I'd say, 'Mr. Russell, there *has* been a voice from heaven; it has predicted many things; and we've seen them undeniably come to pass.'"[26]

Geisler was referring to the miraculous way prophets foretold specific events and circumstances that would culminate hundreds of years later in the Messiah (the "Anointed One") who would redeem Israel and the world. Even a hardened skeptic like Russell recognized that it would take an act of God for someone to make clear predictions of unlikely events and have them fulfilled at a future date against all mathematical odds. Thus, the messianic prophecies that came to pass in Jesus of Nazareth are a powerful confirmation of his identity.

The Old Testament contains scores of prophecies about the coming of the Messiah. *Barton Payne's Encyclopedia of Biblical Prophecy* lists 191 of them, while Oxford scholar Alfred Edersheim cites 400. "The most important point here is to keep in mind the organic *unity* of the Old Testament," Edersheim noted. "Its predictions are not isolated, but features of one grand prophetic picture."[27]

Unquestionably, these predictions were written hundreds of years before Jesus was born in Bethlehem. "Even the most liberal critics admit that the prophetic books were completed some 400 years before Christ, and the Book of Daniel by about 167 B.C.," Geisler said. He added that there's good evidence for dating most of the books considerably earlier than that, with some of the psalms and earlier prophets dating from the eighth and ninth centuries before Christ.[28]

Geisler pointed out that one passage alone, Isaiah 53:2–12, foretells twelve aspects of Christ's passion, all of which were fulfilled—he would be rejected, be a man of sorrow, live a life of suffering, be despised by others, carry our sorrow, be smitten and afflicted by God, be pierced for our transgressions, be wounded for our sins, would suffer like a lamb, would die with the wicked, would be sinless, and would pray for others.

Most rabbis today reject the notion that Isaiah 53 was foreshadowing the Messiah, insisting instead that he was referring to the Jewish nation. However, Geisler said, "It was common for Jewish interpreters before the time of Christ to teach that Isaiah here spoke of the Jewish Messiah. Only after early Christians began using the text apologetically with great force did it become in rabbinical teaching an expression of the suffering Jewish nation. This view is implausible in the context."[29]

Some of the other major predictions about the Messiah, all of which were fulfilled in Jesus, was that he would be born of a woman (Genesis 3:15) who would be a virgin (Isaiah 7:14), of the seed of Abraham (Genesis 12:1–3; 22:18), of the tribe of Judah (Genesis 49:10), of the house of David (2 Samuel 7:12–16), in Bethlehem (Micah 5:2); he would be heralded by the Lord's messenger (Isaiah 40:3); he would cleanse the temple (Malachi 3:1); he would be "cut off" 483 years after the declaration to reconstruct Jerusalem in 444 B.C. (Daniel 9:24–27); he would be rejected (Psalm 118:22); he would have his hands and feet pierced (Psalm 22:16); he would be pierced in his side (Zechariah 12:10); he would rise from the dead (Psalm 16:10); he would ascend into heaven (Psalm 68:18); and he would sit down at the right hand of God (Psalm 110:1).[30]

The exact fulfillment of so many specific predictions is such a persuasive apologetic that critics have repeatedly raised objections to try to negate them. The most common are the following.

Jesus fulfilled the prophecies by accident. The odds against Jesus fulfilling the prophecies by accident would be staggering. In fact, Professor Peter Stoner, who was chairman of Westmont College's science division in the mid 1950s, worked with six hundred students to come up with their best estimate of the mathematical probability of just eight New Testament prophecies being fulfilled in any one person living down to the present time. Taking all eight prophecies together, Stoner then calculated the odds at one chance in a hundred million billion.[31] This is equivalent to the number of one-and-a-half-inch squares it would take to tile every bit of dry land on the planet.

People can disagree with the estimates the students came up with for Stoner's calculations. After all, prophecies can be difficult to quantify, and assessments may differ. Stoner challenged skeptics to come up with their own estimates and run the numbers themselves. But when I examined the prophecies myself, I had to agree with Stoner's conclusion: The chances of anyone coincidentally fulfilling these ancient predictions would surely be prohibitive.

"The odds alone say it would be impossible for anyone to fulfill the Old Testament prophecies. Yet Jesus—and only Jesus throughout all of history—managed to do it," said Louis Lapides, who grew up in a conservative Jewish home but became a Christian and later a pastor after studying the prophecies.[32]

Jesus intentionally fulfilled the prophecies. Although Jesus could have maneuvered his life to fulfill certain prophecies, many of them would have been completely beyond his ability to control, such as his place of birth, his ancestry, his being betrayed for thirty pieces of silver, his method of execution, his legs remaining unbroken on the cross, and soldiers gambling for his clothing.

Gospels writers fabricated details. Some critics maintain that the Gospels simply changed details to make it appear that Jesus fulfilled prophecies when he really didn't. Louis Lapides offers this defense: "When the

Gospels were being circulated, there were people living who had been around when all these things happened. Someone would have said to Matthew, 'You know it didn't happen that way. We're trying to communicate a life of righteousness and truth, so don't taint it with a lie.'" Besides, asked Lapides, why would Matthew fabricate fulfilled prophecies and then willingly allow himself to be put to death for following someone he knew was really not the Messiah? And what's more, although the Talmud refers to Jesus in derogatory ways, it never claims that the fulfillment of prophecies was falsified.[33]

The Gospels misinterpret the prophecies. Matthew reports that Jesus' parents took him to Egypt and then to Nazareth after Herod's death, "and so was fulfilled what the Lord had said through the prophet: 'Out of Egypt I called my son'" (Matthew 2:15). But critics point out that this Old Testament reference was about the children of Israel coming out of Egypt at the exodus. This, they charge, is an example of misinterpreting the intent of the prophets to falsely claim that Jesus fulfilled their predictions.

"The New Testament did apply certain Old Testament passages to Jesus that were not directly predictive of him," Norm Geisler explained. "Many scholars see these references as being 'typologically' fulfilled in Christ. . . . In other words, some truth in the passage can appropriately be applied to Christ even though it was not specifically predictive of him. Other scholars say there's a generic meaning in certain Old Testament passages that apply to both Israel and Christ, both of whom were called God's 'son.' This is sometimes called a 'double-reference view' of prophecy."[34]

Many psychics have successfully predicted the future. A careful study of the track record of psychics, ranging from Nostradamus to Jeane Dixon, shows that, unlike biblical prophecies, their predictions are extremely vague, sometimes contradictory, and very often turn out to be false. Dixon is remembered for predicting John Kennedy's election in 1960, but people forget she later predicted that Richard Nixon would win! One analysis of prophecies by twenty-five psychics showed that 92 percent were totally wrong—unlike the biblical prophets who are invariably right.[35]

Jesus' miraculous fulfillment of the ancient prophecies remains one of the most potent arguments in confirming his identity. Those who carefully scrutinize the record find that these predictions simply cannot be explained away. One of my favorite examples involves Dr. Peter Greenspan, a Jewish obstetrician-gynecologist who also teaches at a medical school. The more he read books by critics who were trying to attack the prophecies, the more he recognized the flaws in their arguments. Ironically, concluded Greenspan, "I think I actually came to faith in Y'shua [Jesus] by reading what detractors wrote."[36]

DID JESUS RISE FROM THE DEAD?

When Christians are asked to provide evidence that their beliefs are grounded in truth rather than legend or wishful thinking, they invariably point to the resurrection of Jesus. The reasons, said J. I. Packer, professor emeritus at Regent College, are numerous and critically important:

> The Easter event, so they affirm, demonstrated Jesus' deity; validated his teaching; attested the completion of his work of atonement for sin; confirms his present cosmic dominion and his coming reappearance as Judge; assures us that his personal pardon, presence, and power in people's lives today is fact; and guarantees each believer's own reembodiment by Resurrection in the world to come.[37]

With so much hinging on the reality of Jesus' return from the dead, it is encouraging to know that this supernatural event is so thoroughly documented in the historical record. Even the once-doubting Sir Lionel Luckhoo, identified by the *Guinness Book of World Records* as the most successful attorney in the world, was forced to conclude after an exhaustive analysis of the evidence, "I say unequivocally that the evidence for the resurrection of Jesus Christ is so overwhelming that it compels acceptance by proof which leaves absolutely no room for doubt."[38]

The evidence begins with the death of Jesus by means of a brutal flogging and crucifixion. The record belies theories that he may have merely swooned on the cross, later to be revived by the cool air of the tomb.

"Clearly, the weight of the historical and medical evidence indicates that Jesus was dead before the wound to his side was inflicted," said an authoritative article in the prestigious *Journal of the American Medical Association*. "Accordingly, interpretations based on the assumption that Jesus did not die on the cross appear to be at odds with modern medical knowledge."[39]

And despite John Dominic Crossan's suggestion on the Jennings documentary (see page 124) that Jesus' body was probably left on the cross "for the carrion, crows, and the prowling dogs," the late liberal scholar John A.T. Robinson of Cambridge University called Jesus' burial "one of the earliest and best-attested facts about Jesus."[40]

The affirmative case for Jesus' resurrection has been described at length in numerous books and scholarly journals. The following four points, however, provide an overview of why, as William Lane Craig said with characteristic understatement, "the sort of skepticism expressed by members of the Jesus Seminar ... not only fails to represent the consensus of scholarship, but is quite unjustified."[41]

Early Accounts: The Trustworthy Testimony of History

The earliest report of Jesus' resurrection goes back so close to the event itself that it cannot have been rendered unreliable by legendary development. In 1 Corinthians 15:3–8, Paul records a critically important creed that was recited by the earliest Christians. It confirms

> that Christ died for our sins according to the Scriptures, that he was buried, that he was raised on the third day according to the Scriptures, and that he appeared to Peter, and then to the Twelve. After that, he appeared to more than five hundred of the brothers at the same time, most of whom are still living, though some have fallen asleep. Then he appeared to James, then to all the apostles, and last of all he appeared to me also, as to one abnormally born.

Scholars from a wide theological spectrum have dated this creed to within two to eight years of Jesus' resurrection, when Paul received it in either Damascus or Jerusalem. Said resurrection expert Gary Habermas, "I would concur with scholars who believe Paul received this material three years after his conversion, when he took a trip to Jerusalem and . . . got it directly from the eyewitnesses Peter and James themselves."[42]

A number of the accounts in Acts 1–5, 10, and 13 also include some creeds that report very early data about Jesus' death and resurrection. "The earliest evidence we have for the resurrection almost certainly goes back to the time immediately after the resurrection event is alleged to have taken place," notes scholar John Drane. "This is the evidence contained in the early sermons in the Acts of the Apostles. . . . There can be no doubt that in the first few chapters of Acts its author has preserved material from very early sources."[43]

In addition, there is evidence that Mark got his passion narrative from an earlier source that was written before A.D. 37, just four years after Jesus' resurrection.[44] These reports from the very front lines of history, coupled with the credible accounts in the other Gospels, demolish contentions that Jesus' resurrection was the result of legendary development that took place in the decades after Jesus' life.

Empty Tomb: It's Unanimous — The Body Is Missing

The vacant tomb, which is reported or implied in the early sources of Mark's Gospel and the 1 Corinthians 15 creed, was conceded by everybody. Not even the Roman authorities or Jewish leaders claimed the tomb still contained Jesus' body. Instead, they were forced to invent the absurd story that the disciples, despite having no motive or opportunity, had stolen the body—a theory that not even the most skeptical critic believes today.

The authenticity of the empty tomb is bolstered by the fact that it was discovered by women, whose testimony was considered so unreliable in first-century Jewish culture that they couldn't testify in a court of law. "This would have been embarrassing for the disciples to admit," observes William Lane Craig, "and most certainly would have been covered up if this were a legend." Craig cites another persuasive fact: "The site of Jesus' tomb was known to Christian and Jew alike. So if it weren't empty, it would be impossible for a movement founded on belief in the Resurrection to have come into existence in the same city where this man had been publicly executed and buried."[45]

Eyewitness Testimony: Seeing Is Believing

Not only was Jesus' tomb empty, but the New Testament reports that over a period of forty days Jesus appeared alive a dozen different times to more than 515 individuals—to men and women, to believers and doubters, to tough-minded people and tenderhearted souls, to groups, to individuals, sometimes indoors and sometimes outdoors in broad daylight.

The Gospels report that Jesus talked with people, ate with them, and even invited one skeptic to put his finger into the nail holes in his hands and to put his hand into the spear wound in his side, to verify it was really him. This experience was so life-changing that church history tells us Thomas ended up proclaiming until his violent death in south India that Jesus had in fact been resurrected.

C. H. Dodd of Cambridge University has carefully analyzed the historical record and concluded that several of these appearances are based on especially early material, including Jesus' encounter with the women in Matthew 28:8–10, his meeting with the eleven apostles in Matthew 28:16–20, and his meeting with the disciples in John 20:19–23.[46]

Critics have charged that these appearances were the result of hallucinations or "group think," where people talk each other into seeing something that isn't there. However, psychologists have convincingly dismissed those possibilities by demonstrating that hallucinations are individual events that cannot be experienced by a crowd and that conditions were not appropriate for "group think" to have occurred.[47] Besides, if the disciples only imagined Jesus appearing to them alive, where did the body go?

Suggestions that the idea of the risen Jesus was taken from ancient mythology involving dying and rising gods also fall short when these legendary stories are seen in their proper context as expressions of the cycle of nature, whereby crops die in the fall and come to life in the spring. "Contrast that with the depiction of Jesus Christ in the gospels," says Gregory Boyd, author of *Cynic Sage or Son of God?* "That's concrete historical stuff. It has nothing in common with stories about what supposedly happened 'once upon a time.'"[48]

Theologian and historian Carl Braaten makes this observation: "Even the more skeptical historians agree that for primitive Christianity . . . the resurrection of Jesus from the dead was a real event in history, the very foundation of faith, and not a mythical idea arising out of the creative imagination of believers."[49]

Emergence of the Church: Filling a Hole in History

J. P. Moreland has observed that it would have taken something as dramatic as Jesus' resurrection to prompt first-century Jews to switch from Saturday to Sunday worship, to abandon both the system of sacrificing animals for forgiveness of sins and adhering to the laws of Moses as a way to maintain right standing with God, and to embrace the concept of the Trinity. In doing so, those who started the church risked becoming social outcasts and, according to Jewish theology, having their souls damned to hell.

"How could such a thing ever take place?" Moreland asks. "The Resurrection offers the only rational explanation."[50]

Thus the famous quote from C. F. D. Moule, New Testament scholar from Cambridge University: "If the coming into existence of the [church], a phenomenon undeniably attested by the New Testament, rips a great hole in history, a hole the size and shape of Resurrection, what does the secular historian propose to stop it up with?"[51]

Consider the most extreme examples of life change after the resurrection. James was a skeptic of Jesus while Jesus was alive; Saul of Tarsus persecuted Christians. What else except their encounter with the risen Christ could have transformed them into leaders of the early church who were willing to die for their conviction that Jesus is the Son of God? As for Jesus' disciples, they went from cowering in fear after the death of Jesus to suddenly proclaiming, boldly and powerfully, that Jesus proved he is God by overcoming the grave.

"The radically changed behavior of the disciples after the resurrection is the best evidence of the resurrection," declares Thomas C. Oden of Drew University. "Some hypothesis is necessary to make plausible the transformation of the disciples from grieving followers of a crucified messiah to those whose resurrection preaching turned the world upside down. That change could not have happened, according to the church's testimony, without the risen Lord."[52]

When I personally ponder Jesus' question, "Who do you say I am?" (Matthew 16:15), these five broad categories of evidence—the reliability of the New Testament, Jesus' supreme self-understanding, his miracles, his fulfillment of prophecy, and his resurrection—immediately come to my mind. To me the record is clear. Jesus is an actual figure of history, whose convicting and comforting words and whose awe-inspiring and compassionate deeds have been reliably preserved for us in the Gospels. He is someone who not only saw himself in transcendent, divine, and messianic terms, but who also fulfilled all the attributes that make God, God.

Jesus is a worker of miracles, a loving healer of the blind and lame, whose supernatural feats heralded the inbreaking of the kingdom of God. He is the much-anticipated Messiah through whom God brought redemption and hope to Israel and the world. And he is the resurrected Lord, whose empty tomb gives his followers rock-solid confidence that as he has overcome the grave, so they will also.

If you are a spiritual seeker, my hope is that you will sincerely consider the evidence for yourself and then have the courage to respond to it by receiving Jesus as your forgiver and leader. If you are already a Christian, then you also have a task before you—to articulate the truth about Christ, to defend it, to share it, to preserve it, to pass it along to the next generations. As J. B. Phillips so powerfully renders 2 Corinthians 4:6: "God, who first ordered light to shine in darkness, has flooded our hearts with his light, so that we can enlighten men with the knowledge of the glory of God, as we see it in the face of Christ."

QUESTIONS FOR REFLECTION AND DISCUSSION

1. If someone claimed to be the Son of God, what kind of evidence would you want to corroborate his assertion? How well do you think Jesus' miracles, fulfillment of prophecies, and resurrection confirm his identity? Which of these categories of evidence do you find most convincing? Why?

2. The disciples were in a unique position of knowing for certain whether Jesus had returned from the dead, and they were willing to die for their conviction that he did. Can you think of anyone in history who has knowingly and willingly died for a lie? What degree of certainty would you need before you would be willing to lay down your life for a belief? How thoroughly would you investigate a matter if you were going to base your life on it? What does this tell you about the persuasiveness of the disciples' testimony?

3. What explanation other than Jesus' resurrection could account for the empty tomb, the sightings of the once-dead Jesus, and the radically changed behavior of the disciples? How do you think the scholars quoted in this chapter would respond to your hypothesis? If the resurrection is true, what does this mean personally for you?

Chapter 6

TOUGH QUESTIONS ABOUT THE BIBLE

NORMAN GEISLER

Most church members (and even many pastors) are not formally trained in defending the Faith (apologetics) and hence cannot always answer tough questions they are asked. Nevertheless, the Bible commands us, "Let your conversation be always full of grace, seasoned with salt, so that you may know how to answer everyone" (Colossians 4:6). Peter urged, "Always be prepared to give an answer to everyone who asks you to give the reason for the hope that you have" (1 Peter 3:15). These are commands to all believers, not just Christian leaders. The apostle Paul insisted that church leaders "must hold firmly to the trustworthy message as it has been taught, so that [they] can encourage others by sound doctrine and refute those who oppose it" (Titus 1:9).

In an age of increasing skepticism, agnosticism, and cultism, we are called on all the more to get answers to the questions being asked. This is true not only for outsiders to whom we witness, but even for fellow members who themselves have unanswered questions about the faith. One of the areas most under attack is our belief in the Bible as God's Word. Here are brief answers to some of the tough questions being asked.

Questions about the Origin of the Bible

Evangelicals believe that the Scriptures came from God through men of God who wrote down the very words of God.[1] That is, the Bible has a divine origin, even though it was produced through human instrumentality. But this belief occasions many questions from our culture. The following are a select group of often asked questions.

WHERE DID THE BIBLE COME FROM?

The Bible claims to have come from God. Speaking of the whole Old Testament, Paul wrote, "All Scripture is God-breathed and is useful for teaching, rebuking, correcting and training in righteousness" (2 Timothy 3:16). Even the New Testament is called Scripture. Paul cited the gospel as "Scripture" in 1 Timothy 5:18. And Peter referred to Paul's epistles as Scripture in 2 Peter 3:15–16. So both the entire Old and New Testament, both Gospels and Epistles, are said to be writings that are "breathed out" by God. Jesus used a similar expression when he referred to the Word of God coming out of the "mouth of God," saying to the tempter, "Man does not live on bread alone, but on every word that comes from the mouth of God" (Matthew 4:4).

WHO WROTE THE BIBLE?

Not only does the Bible claim to be a God-breathed writing, but it comes from Spirit-moved writers. Peter referred to the Old Testament prophets as men who were "carried along" by the Holy Spirit. "For prophecy never came by the will of man, but holy men of God spoke as they were moved by the Holy Spirit" (2 Peter 1:21 NKJV). David added, "The Spirit of the LORD spoke through me; his word was on my tongue" (2 Samuel 23:2). So the Bible claims to have come from God through men of God.

The Bible was written by prophets of God. God is the ultimate source of the Bible, but men of God called prophets were the instruments God used to record his words. The role of biblical prophets was unique. They were the mouthpieces of God, commissioned to speak his words, nothing more and nothing less (Proverbs 30:6; Revelation 22:18–19). God told

Balaam, "Speak only what I tell you" (Numbers 22:35). Balaam responded, "Can I say just anything? I must speak only what God puts in my mouth" (verse 38). As Amos put it, "The Sovereign LORD has spoken—who can but prophesy?" (Amos 3:8).

The whole Old Testament was written by prophets. Some Old Testament writers were prophets by *office*. Moses was a prophet (Deuteronomy 18:15). He wrote the first five books of the Bible known as "the book of Moses" (Mark 12:26) or "Moses" (Luke 24:27). All the books after him were at first called "the Prophets" (Matthew 5:17; Luke 24:27). The New Testament refers to the whole Old Testament as a prophetic writing (2 Peter 1:20–21; cf. Hebrews 1:1). Beginning with Samuel (1 Samuel 10:10–12) there was a company of the prophets (1 Samuel 19:20). Some men such as Elijah (1 Kings 18:36; Malachi 4:5) or Elisha (2 Kings 9:1) were known as prophets.

Other Old Testament writers were prophets by *gift*. That is, they did not belong to the group or company of prophets, but God spoke to them and gave them a message to deliver to the people (Amos 7:14–15). Daniel was a prince by profession (Daniel 1:3–6), but he became a prophet by calling and gift. Jesus called him "the prophet Daniel" (Matthew 24:15). David was a shepherd boy, but God spoke to him. David wrote, "The Spirit of the LORD spoke through me; his word was on my tongue" (2 Samuel 23:2). Even Solomon, who wrote Proverbs, Ecclesiastes, and Song of Songs, received revelations from God as a prophet does (1 Kings 3:5). The rest of the Old Testament authors fit into this category, since their writings were in the section known as "the Prophets" (Matthew 5:17; Luke 24:27) and since the Old Testament was known as a prophetic writing (Hebrews 1:1; 2 Peter 1:20–21).

Likewise, all the New Testament writers were "apostles and prophets," since the church was built on this foundation (Ephesians 2:20). They, too, claimed to receive their message from God. Paul, who wrote about half of the New Testament books, was considered to have written inspired Scripture in the same category as the Old Testament (2 Peter 3:15–16). Matthew and John were among those Jesus promised to lead into "all truth" and bring to their remembrance whatever he taught them (John 16:13; 14:26). Peter, one of the chief apostles, wrote two books based on his credentials as an apostle and eyewitness of Jesus (see 1 Peter 1:1; 2 Peter 1:1, 16). The other New Testament writers were associates of the apostles and prophets by gift, since God spoke through these servants of Jesus as well (see James 1:1; Jude 1–3).

WERE THE BIBLICAL AUTHORS MERE SECRETARIES OF THE HOLY SPIRIT?

The biblical authors did not simply take dictation from God. They were not mere secretaries or automatons, but they were faithful to proclaim the whole message from God without adding to it or taking away from it (Proverbs 30:6; Revelation 22:18–19). God used the individual personalities, vocabularies, literary styles, and conscious desires of the biblical authors to produce his Word. Thus, while being completely from God, the words of Scripture are also human words in particular human languages (Hebrew, Greek, and Aramaic) expressed in distinctive human literary forms that include narrative (Samuel), poetry (Psalms), and parables (Gospels), as well as metaphor (John 15:1–8), some allegory (Galatians 4:21–5:1), and even hyperbole (Psalm 6:6; Luke 14:26). Nonetheless, the final product is exactly as God ordained and providentially superintended it to be—the divinely authoritative, infallible, and inerrant Word of God. For the Scripture "cannot be broken" (John 10:35) or "disappear" (Matthew 5:18). It is the "truth" (John 17:17) that comes from a God for whom "it is impossible . . . to lie" (Hebrews 6:18). In short, it is without error in whatever it affirms, not only on spiritual matters, but also on science (see Matthew 19:12; John 3:12) and history (see Matthew 12:40–42; 24:37).[2] In short, the biblical writers were humans God chose to be his mouthpiece through the use of human language and literary forms.[3]

WHAT WAS A PROPHET IN BIBLE TIMES?

The biblical authors were prophets and apostles of God. Many designations of prophets give information about their role in producing Scripture. Some roles listed are:

- man of God (1 Kings 12:22), meaning that he was chosen by God
- the Lord's servant (1 Kings 14:18), indicating that he was faithful to God
- the Lord's messenger (Isaiah 42:19), showing that he was sent by God
- seer, or beholder (Isaiah 30:10), revealing that his insight was from God
- man of the Spirit (Hosea 9:7 KJV; cf. Micah 3:8), telling that he spoke by the Spirit of God
- watchman (Ezekiel 3:17), reflecting his alertness for God
- prophet (which he is most commonly called), marking him as a spokesman for God

In short, a prophet is a mouthpiece of God. He is someone God chooses, prepares, and uses as his instrument to convey his word to his people.

COULD PROPHETS ADD THEIR PERSONAL THOUGHTS TO GOD'S MESSAGE?

No, they were forbidden to do so. God said, "Do not add to what I command you and do not subtract from it" (Deuteronomy 4:2). Jeremiah was commanded: "This is what the LORD says: Stand in the courtyard of the LORD's house and speak to all the people. . . . Tell them everything I command you; do not omit a word" (Jeremiah 26:2).

The nature of a biblical prophet guaranteed that he would not add his thoughts to God's message, for he is one who speaks "everything the LORD had said" (Exodus 4:30). God said to Moses of a prophet, "I will put my words in his mouth, and he will tell them everything I command him" (Deuteronomy 18:18). And Amos wrote, "The Sovereign LORD has spoken—who can but prophesy?" (Amos 3:8). In brief, a prophet was someone who said what God told him to say, no more and no less.

The very nature of a prophet demanded that a prophetic writing is exactly what God wants to say to mankind. And since the Bible is presented as a prophetic writing from beginning to end (Matthew 5:17–18; 2 Peter 1:20–21; Revelation 22:9), it follows that the written record of the prophets was considered inspired by God. Indeed, this is what the prophet Zechariah declared when he wrote, "They made their hearts as hard as flint and would not listen to the law or to the words that the LORD Almighty had sent by his Spirit through the earlier prophets. So the LORD Almighty was very angry" (Zechariah 7:12).

HOW DID PROPHETS GET THEIR MESSAGES FROM GOD?

The prophets received their messages from God in various ways. Some received them in dreams (Genesis 37:1–11), others in visions (Daniel 7), and some even by an audible voice (1 Samuel 3) or an inner voice (Hosea 1; Joel 1). Others received revelations from angels (Genesis 19:1–29), some by way of miracles (Exodus 3), and others by way of the lot (Proverbs 16:33). The high priest used jewels known as the Urim and Thummim (Exodus 28:30). God spoke to still others as they meditated on his revelation in nature (Psalm 8; 19:1–6). Whatever the means, as the author of Hebrews put it, "In the past God spoke to our forefathers through the prophets at many times and in various ways" (Hebrews 1:1).

WERE THE PROPHETS PERMITTED TO CHANGE THE WORDS GOD GAVE?

Biblical prophets were forbidden to tamper with the text of sacred Scripture. God dealt severely with anyone who attempted to change his words. After King Jehoiakim cut out and burned section after section from the words of the Lord, Jeremiah was told: "Take another scroll and write on it all the words that were on the first scroll" (Jeremiah 36:28). No one was to add to or take away from what God had said. Agur wrote, "Every word of God is flawless. . . . Do not add to his words, or he will rebuke you and prove you a liar" (Proverbs 30:5–6). Indeed, John wrote this about the words of his prophecy: "If anyone adds anything to them, God will add to him the plagues described in this book. And if anyone takes words away from this book of prophecy, God will take away from him his share in the tree of life" (Revelation 22:18–19). This didn't mean that they could not receive new revelations, but that they could not tamper with old ones.

Questions about the Nature of the Bible

Since the Bible claims to come from God, it asserts a divine authority. It claims to be the very word of God (John 10:34–35). But since the Bible was also written by human beings, just what is meant when we call it "God's Word"?

WHAT DO YOU MEAN WHEN YOU SAY "THE BIBLE IS THE WORD OF GOD"?

Since God is the source of the Bible, it is appropriate to call it his Word. But since human writers composed every word in the Bible, it is also true that it is their word. Hence, one way to describe what is meant when the Bible claims to be "God-breathed" (2 Timothy 3:16) is this: "What the Bible says, God says." This is manifested in the fact that often an Old Testament passage will claim that God said it, yet when this same text is cited in the New Testament, it asserts that "the Scripture(s)" said it. And sometimes the reverse is true, namely, in the Old Testament it is the Bible that records it, but the New Testament declares that it was God who said it: Consider these comparisons:

What God Says ...	the Bible Says
Genesis 12:3	Galatians 3:8
Exodus 9:13, 16	Romans 9:17

In Genesis God is speaking: "The LORD had said to Abram, 'Leave your country, your people and your father's household and go to the land I will show you. . . . I will bless those who bless you, and whoever curses you I will curse; and all peoples on earth will be blessed through you'" (Genesis 12:1–3). But when this is cited in Galatians 3:8, we read, "The Scripture . . . announced the gospel in advance to Abraham: 'All nations will be blessed through you.'"

Likewise in Exodus 9:13, 16: "Then the LORD said to Moses, 'Get up early in the morning, confront Pharaoh and say to him, "This is what the LORD, the God of the Hebrews says: Let my people go, so that they may worship me. . . . I have raised you up for this very purpose, that I might show you my power and that my name might be proclaimed in all the earth."'" However, when the New Testament quotes this passage, it says: "For the Scripture says to Pharaoh: 'I raised you up for this very purpose, that I might display my power in you and that my name might be proclaimed in all the earth'" (Romans 9:17).

What the Bible Says . . . God Says

Genesis 2:24	Matthew 19:4–5
Psalm 2:1	Acts 4:24–25
Isaiah 55:3	Acts 13:34
Psalm 16:10	Acts 13:35
Psalm 2:7	Hebrews 1:5

In the book of Genesis we read, "For this reason a man will leave his father and mother and be united to his wife, and they will become one flesh" (Genesis 2:24). When this is cited by Jesus in the New Testament, he said, "Haven't you read that at the beginning [God] the Creator . . . said, 'For this reason a man will leave his father and mother and be united to his wife, and the two will become one flesh'?" (Matthew 19:4–5).

The same is true in Psalm 2:1 in the Old Testament, where it is David who wrote, "Why do the nations conspire, and the peoples plot in vain?" but when this is cited in the New Testament, we read, "When they heard this, they raised their voices together in prayer to God. 'Sovereign Lord, . . . You spoke by the Holy Spirit through the mouth of your servant, our father David: "Why do the nations rage and the peoples plot in vain?"'" (Acts 4:24–25).

Noted theologian B. B. Warfield made this observation: "In one of these classes of passages the Scriptures are spoken of as if they were God; in the other, God is spoken of as if He were the Scriptures. . . . In the two taken together, God and the Scriptures are brought into such conjunction as to show that in point of directness of authority no distinction was made between them."[4]

HOW ELSE DOES THE BIBLE CLAIM TO BE THE WORD OF GOD?

By means of phrases such as "says the LORD" (e.g., Isaiah 1:11, 18), "declares the LORD" (e.g., Jeremiah 2:3, 9), "God said" (e.g., Genesis 1:3, 6), "this word came to Jeremiah from the LORD" (Jeremiah 34:1), and "The word of the LORD came to me" (e.g., Ezekiel 30:1), the Scriptures claim to come from God. Such phrases are found hundreds of times in Scripture and reveal beyond question that the writer is affirming that he records the very word of God. In the book of Leviticus alone there are some sixty-six occurrences of phrases like "the LORD said to Moses" (e.g., 4:1; 5:14; 6:1, 8, 19; 7:22). Ezekiel records countless times phrases like "I saw visions" or "the word of the LORD came to me." Five times in twenty-eight verses of chapter 12, Ezekiel says, "The word of the LORD came to me" (verses 1, 8, 17, 21, 26), and four times he writes, "This is what the Sovereign LORD says" (verses 10, 19, 23, 28). And in verse 28 he uses the combination "This is what the Sovereign LORD says" and "declares the Sovereign LORD" (cf. 20:3). Isaiah (e.g., 1:1, 11, 18, 24; 2:1), Jeremiah (e.g., 1:2, 13; 2:1, 3, 5), and other prophets make similar statements. The overall impression leaves no doubt as to the confessed source in God himself of the messages of the prophets.

DOES THE BIBLE ACTUALLY CLAIM TO BE THE "WORD OF GOD" IN SO MANY WORDS?

Yes, it does. Many times the Bible claims to be "the Word of God" in these very words or their equivalent. Jesus told some of the Jewish leaders of his day, "Thus you nullify the word of God for the sake of your tradition" (Matthew 15:6). Paul speaks of the Scriptures as "the very words of God" (Romans 3:2). And Peter declares, "For you have been born again, not of perishable seed, but of imperishable, through the living and enduring word of God" (1 Peter 1:23). And the writer of Hebrews affirms, "For the word of God is living and active. Sharper than any double-edged sword, it penetrates even to dividing soul and spirit, joints and marrow; it judges the thoughts and attitudes of the heart" (Hebrews 4:12). Jesus used the phrase "word of God" as equivalent with the Law (Torah) and Scripture, asserting:

"Is it not written in your Law . . . to whom the word of God came—and the Scripture cannot be broken . . ." (John 10:34–35).

DOES THE BIBLE CLAIM TO HAVE DIVINE AUTHORITY?

The Bible uses many other words or phrases to describe itself in ways that validate its divine authority. Jesus said that the Bible is indestructible: "I tell you the truth, until heaven and earth disappear, not the smallest letter, not the least stroke of a pen, will by any means disappear" (Matthew 5:18); it is infallible (completely reliable and authoritative) or "unbreakable" (see John 10:35); it has final and decisive authority (Matthew 4:4, 7, 10), and it is sufficient for faith and practice. Jesus spoke of the sufficiency of the Jewish Scriptures: "If they do not listen to Moses and the Prophets, they will not be convinced even if someone rises from the dead" (Luke 16:31). Paul added, "All Scripture is God-breathed and is useful for teaching, rebuking, correcting and training in righteousness, so that the man of God may be thoroughly equipped for every good work" (2 Timothy 3:16–17).

HOW FAR DOES THIS DIVINE AUTHORITY EXTEND?

The extent of divine authority in Scripture includes all that is written (2 Timothy 3:16), even the very words (Matthew 22:43; 1 Corinthians 2:13)—including even the smallest parts of words (Matthew 5:17–18)—and the tenses of verbs (Matthew 22:32). Even though the Bible was not verbally dictated by God to humans, nonetheless, the result is just as perfect as if it had been. For the biblical authors claimed that God is the source of the very words of Scripture, since he supernaturally superintended the process by which they wrote, using their own vocabulary and style to record God's message (2 Peter 1:20–21).

WHAT DO YOU MEAN WHEN YOU SAY THAT THE BIBLE IS INSPIRED?

Second Timothy 3:16 declares that the Bible is *God-breathed* (KJV, "given by inspiration"): "All Scripture is God-breathed and is useful for teaching, rebuking, correcting and training in righteousness." Jesus said, "Man does not live on bread alone, but on every word that *comes from the mouth of God*" (Matthew 4:4, italics added). Combine this truth with 2 Peter 1:20–21, which affirms that the Scriptures were given by men who "spoke from God as they were carried along by the Holy Spirit," and we see that inspiration as a whole is the process by which Spirit-moved writers produced God-breathed writings.

ARE THE VERY WORDS OF THE BIBLE INSPIRED BY GOD, OR ONLY THE IDEAS?

Numerous Scriptures make it evident that the locus of revelation and inspiration is the written Word—the Scriptures (Greek *grapha*)—not simply the idea or even the writer, but his actual writing. Notice the reference to revealed or divinely inspired "Scripture" (2 Timothy 3:16; 2 Peter 1:20–21), "words taught by the Spirit" (1 Corinthians 2:13), "the Book" (2 Chronicles 34:14), "his [God's] word" (2 Samuel 23:2), "my [God's] words" (Isaiah 59:21), and "the words that the LORD Almighty had sent" (Zechariah 7:12).

When referring to the Old Testament as the authoritative Word of God, the New Testament most often (more than ninety times) uses the phrase "it is written" (e.g., Matthew 4:4, 7, 10). Jesus described this written word as that which "comes from the mouth of God" (Matthew 4:4). So important were the exact words of God that Jeremiah was told: "This is what the LORD says: Stand in the courtyard of the LORD's house and speak to all the people of the towns of Judah who come to worship in the house of the LORD. Tell them everything I command you; do not omit a word" (Jeremiah 26:2). So it was not simply that men were free to state God's word in their own words; the very choice of words was from God. Exodus 24:4 records that "Moses then wrote down everything the LORD had said." In Deuteronomy, Moses writes, "I [God] will raise up for them a prophet like you from among their brothers; I will put my words in his mouth, and he will tell them everything I command him" (Deuteronomy 18:18).

Sometimes God chose to emphasize even the tenses of verbs. Jesus said, "But about the resurrection of the dead—have you not read what God said to you, 'I am [not was] the God of Abraham, the God of Isaac, and the God of Jacob'? He is not the God of the dead but of the living" (Matthew 22:31–32). Paul based his argument on a singular versus a plural noun in Galatians 3:16, insisting, "Scripture does not say 'and to seeds,' meaning many people, but 'and to your seed,' meaning one person, who is Christ."

Even one letter (the letter *s,* for example) can make a big difference. Jesus went so far as to declare that even parts of letters are inspired. In English, if a *t* is not crossed, it can look like an *i.* Thus, Jesus said, "I tell you the truth, until heaven and earth disappear, not the smallest letter, not the least stroke of a pen, will by any means disappear from the Law until everything is accomplished" (Matthew 5:18).

DOES THE BIBLE CLAIM TO BE INSPIRED ON ALL TOPICS OR JUST SPIRITUAL ONES?

Inspiration does guarantee the truth of everything the Bible teaches, implies, or entails (spiritually or factually). Paul affirmed that *all Scripture,* not just some, is God-breathed (2 Timothy 3:16). Peter declared that *no prophecy* of Scripture comes from man but it all comes from God (2 Peter 1:20–21). Jesus told his disciples, "The Counselor, the Holy Spirit, whom the Father will send in my name, will teach you all things and will remind you of everything I have said to you" (John 14:26). In this same discourse he added, "When he, the Spirit of truth, comes, he will guide you into all truth" (John 16:13).

The church is "built on the foundation of the apostles and prophets, with Christ Jesus himself as the chief cornerstone" (Ephesians 2:20). And the early church "devoted themselves to the apostles' teaching" (Acts 2:42), recorded for us in the pages of the New Testament, which was considered to be sacred Scripture along with the Old Testament (cf. 1 Timothy 5:18, where an Old and New Testament text are cited; 2 Peter 3:15–16).

The inspiration of God, then, extends to every part of Scripture. It includes everything God affirmed (or denied) about any topic included in Scripture. It is inclusive of not only what the Bible teaches explicitly but also what it teaches implicitly. It covers not only spiritual matters but factual ones as well. The all-knowing God cannot be wrong about anything

he teaches or implies. Indeed, Jesus verified historical and scientific matters, including the creation of Adam and Eve (Matthew 19:4–5), the flood
during Noah's time (Matthew 24:37–39), and even Jonah being swallowed
by a great fish (Matthew 12:40–42). Indeed, Jesus said, "I have spoken to
you of earthly things and you do not believe; how, then, will you believe if
I speak of heavenly things" (John 3:12).

HOW DO SOME PEOPLE MISUNDERSTAND WHAT IS MEANT BY THE INSPIRATION OF THE BIBLE?

The Bible is inspired by God with regard to everything it teaches.
There are, however, a number of common misunderstandings:

- that every part of a parable has to convey a fact rather than help the parable illustrate its point (see Luke 18:2)
- that everything it records is true rather than something merely taught or implied (Genesis 3:4)
- that no exaggerations (hyperboles) are used (Psalm 6:6; Luke 14:26)
- that all statements about God and creation are purely literal (Job 38:7; Hebrews 4:13)
- that all factual assertions are technically precise by modern standards as opposed to accurate by ancient standards (2 Chronicles 4:2)
- that all statements about the universe must come out of a modern astronomical perspective as opposed to a common observational standpoint (Joshua 10:12)
- that all citations of Scripture must be verbatim as opposed to faithful to the meaning (Psalm 2:1 and Acts 4:25)
- that all citations of Scripture must have the same application as the original (Hosea 11:1 and Matthew 2:15) rather than the same interpretation (meaning)
- that the same truth can be said in only one way as opposed to many ways, as it is in the Gospels

- that whatever a writer personally believed, as opposed to merely what he actually affirmed in Scripture, is true (Matthew 15:26)
- that truth is exhaustively revealed or treated as opposed to adequately presented in the Bible (1 Corinthians 13:12)
- that quotations imply the truth of everything in the source it is citing rather than just the part cited (Titus 1:12)
- that a particular grammatical construction will always be the customary one rather than an adequate one to convey the truth[5]

HOW DO WE KNOW THESE MISUNDERSTANDINGS AREN'T PART OF WHAT INSPIRATION COVERS?

What the Bible says must be understood in view of what the Bible shows. What it preaches must be read in view of what it practices. The doctrine of Scripture is to be understood in the light of the data of Scripture. All the misunderstandings listed in the previous question are part of the data of Scripture. For instance, the Bible uses round numbers. Thus, when the Bible claims to be true, it does not mean to exclude the use of round numbers (2 Chronicles 4). The same is true of hyperboles, figures of speech, observational language, and literary genre (as poetry, parable, and the like). In short, everything the Bible affirms is true, but what is meant by truth must be understood in the light of the phenomena or data of Scripture.

ISN'T THE BIBLE ALSO A HUMAN BOOK?

Yes, it is, in fact, 100 percent human. The Bible was written by human authors (including Moses, Joshua, Samuel, David, Isaiah, Jeremiah, Ezekiel, a number of other prophets, Ezra, Nehemiah, Matthew, Mark, Luke, John, Paul, Peter, and others).

The Bible was composed in human languages (Hebrew in the Old Testament and Greek in the New Testament). The Bible is expressed in human literary styles (including the exalted poetry of Isaiah, the mournful lamentations of Jeremiah, the parables of Jesus recorded in the Gospels, and the didactic presentation of Paul.

The Bible uses different human literary forms, including the narrative of Samuel and Kings, the poetry of Job and Psalms, the parables of the synoptic Gospels, some allegory as in Galatians 4, the use of symbols as in Revelation, the metaphors and similes of James, satire (Matthew 19:24), and hyperbole (Psalm 6:6; Luke 14:26). Like other human writing, the Bible uses a wide range of literary forms to convey its meaning.

The Bible reflects different human perspectives. These include a shepherd's perspective (David in Psalm 23), a prophetic vantage point in Kings, a priestly perspective in Chronicles, the historical interest of Luke-Acts (see Luke 1:1–4; Acts 1:1), and the pastoral concerns of Paul (in 1 and 2 Timothy and Titus). And unlike a modern book on astronomy, biblical writers speak from an observer's perspective when they write of the sun rising or setting (Joshua 1:15; cf. 10:13).

The Bible reflects different human thought patterns. These include almost every dimension of finite thinking patterns, from a tightly knit logical treatise like Romans, to the polemics of Galatians, to the expression of a brief memory lapse in 1 Corinthians 1:14–16.

The Bible reveals different human emotions. The apostle Paul expresses great sorrow over Israel (Romans 9:2), great anger over the error of the Galatians (Galatians 3:1), melancholy and loneliness over his imprisonment (2 Timothy 4:9–16), depression over hardships (2 Corinthians 1:8), joy over victories (Philippians 1:4), and much more.

The Bible manifests specific human interests. Luke had a medical interest, as indicated by his use of medical terms. Hosea had a distinct rural interest, as did Amos, the shepherd from Tekoa (Amos 1:1). James's writing betrays an interest in nature (see James 1:6, 10–11). The interests of shepherds (John 10:1–16), athletes (1 Corinthians 9:24–27), and farmers (Matthew 13:1–43) are also reflected in the Bible.

The Bible expresses human culture. As a Semitic book, the Bible is filled with expressions and practices of its Hebrew culture, such as the common means of greeting by kissing (1 Thessalonians 5:26) and a woman's use of a veil as a sign of respect for her husband (1 Corinthians 11:5). Washing one's feet upon entering a home (see John 13), shaking off the dust of one's feet as a sign of condemnation (Luke 10:11), and reclining (not sitting) at meals (John 13:23) are only a few of numerous other examples of human culture.

The Bible utilizes other written human sources. The book of Jashar (Joshua 10:13) and the Books of the Wars of the LORD (Numbers 21:14) are examples. "The records of Samuel the seer, the records of Nathan the prophet and the records of Gad the seer" may also fit in this category (1 Chronicles 29:29). Luke referred to written sources about Jesus available to him (Luke 1:1–4).[6] Paul quoted non-Christian poets three times (Acts 17:28; 1 Corinthians 15:33; Titus 1:12). Jude cited material from the noncanonical books The Testament of Moses and the book of Enoch (Jude 9, 14). These citations do not guarantee the truthfulness of everything in the source but only what is cited. Of course, ultimately all truth comes from God, whatever the immediate source may be.

DOES THE BIBLE HAVE ERRORS IN IT?

The original text of the Bible does not teach any error. The logic of the Bible's errorlessness is straightforward: (1) God cannot err (Titus 1:2; Hebrews 6:18); (2) the Bible is God's Word (John 10:34–35); (3) therefore, the Bible cannot contain error. Since the Scriptures are breathed out by God (2 Timothy 3:16–17) and God cannot breathe out falsehood, it follows that the Bible cannot contain any falsehood.

ARE THERE ERRORS IN BIBLE MANU-SCRIPTS AND TRANSLATIONS?

There are some minor copyist errors in the Bible manuscripts. A couple examples will suffice. The Masoretic Text of 2 Chronicles 22:2 says Ahaziah was forty-two, yet 2 Kings 8:26 asserts that Ahaziah was twenty-two. He could not have been forty-two (a copyist's error), or he would have been older than his father. Also, 2 Chronicles 9:25 affirms that Solomon had four thousand horse stalls, but the Masoretic Text of 1 Kings 4:26 says he had forty thousand horse stalls, which would have been way more than needed for the twelve thousand horsemen he had.

It is important to keep these things in mind with regard to these copyist errors:

- No original manuscript has ever been found with an error in it.
- They are relatively rare.
- In most cases we know which one is wrong from the context or the material found in parallel passages.
- In no case is the doctrine of Scripture affected.
- They vouch for the accuracy of the copying process, since the scribes who copied them knew there were errors in the manuscripts but they were duty-bound to copy what the text said.
- They don't affect the central message of the Bible.

Someone may, in fact, receive a message with errors in it, yet have 100 percent of the message come through clearly. For example, suppose you received a message from Western Union that read as follows: "Y#u have won 20 million dollars."

No doubt you would gladly pick up your money. And if the telegram read in any of the ways that follow, you would have no doubt at all:

- "Yo# have won 20 million dollars."
- "You #ave won 20 million dollars."
- "You h#ve won 20 million dollars."

Why would we be more sure if there are more errors? Because each error is in a different place, and with it we get another confirmation of every other letter in the original message.

Three things are important to note. First, even with one line, error and all, 100 percent of the message comes through. Second, the more lines, the more errors—but the more errors, the more sure we are of what the intended message really was. Finally, there are hundreds of times more Bible manuscripts than there are lines in the above example. And there is a greater percentage of error in this telegram than in all the collated biblical manuscripts.

HOW CAN THE BIBLE BE BOTH GOD'S WORDS AND MAN'S WORDS?

The Bible is both the word of God and the words of man because God (the source) utilized human beings to convey his word. So there is a concurrence between what the human authors wrote and what God prompted them to write.

The Bible is both divine and human at the same time in a way similar to the way Christians believe Jesus Christ is both divine and human at the same time. Both Christ and Scripture are *theanthropic* (Greek *theos* = God; *anthrōpos* = man). This involves major factors:

- Both are called the Word of God. Jesus Christ is the living Word (John 1:1), and the Bible is the written Word (John 10:34–35).
- Each has two natures, one divine and one human.
- The two natures of both are united by one medium. To borrow a term from Christology, both have a kind of "hypostatic union." The two natures of Christ are united in one person. And the two natures of Christ are united in one set of propositions (i.e., sentences).
- Likewise, both Christ and Scripture are without flaw. Christ is without sin (2 Corinthians 5:21; Hebrews 4:15), and the Bible is without error (John 10:35; see John 17:17).

Of course, as in any analogy, there are some differences. Unlike Jesus Christ who is God, the Bible is not God, and hence it should not be worshiped. The difference is that the unifying medium of Christ's two natures is God, the second person of the Godhead. Whereas the unifying factor in the Bible is the human words, wherein there is a divine and human concurrence, in Christ the unity is found in the one Person who is both God and man. Hence, God is to be revered (worshiped), but the Bible should only be respected, not revered.

Questions about the Reliability of the Bible

Evangelicals affirm the reliability of the biblical text from God to us. Can we trust the Bible historically? Is it really a reliable record?[7] Since the historical reliability of the Bible is a crucial link in knowing that the Bible is the Word of God, it is important to address these questions. The reliability of the text of Scripture is determined by two major factors: (1) the reliability of those who wrote it, and (2) the reliability of those who copied it.

WERE THE BIBLICAL WITNESSES RELIABLE?

The biblical witnesses were very reliable for many reasons. First, the writers of Scripture were by and large contemporaries of the events. Moses was a witness of the events in Exodus through Deuteronomy (see Exodus 24:4; Deuteronomy 31:24). Joshua was a witness of the happenings reported in his book (Joshua 24:26), as were Samuel (1 Samuel 10:25), Isaiah, Jeremiah, Daniel, Ezra, and Nehemiah after him. The same is true in the New Testament. Matthew was a disciple of Jesus. Mark was a contemporary and associate of the apostle Peter (1 Peter 5:13). Luke was a contemporary who knew the eyewitnesses (Luke 1:1–4). And John was a disciple of Jesus and eyewitness of the events (1 John 1:1–2).

Second, in the case of the New Testament writers, all eight (or nine)[8] of them were either apostles or associated with the apostles as eyewitnesses and/or contemporaries: Matthew, Mark, Luke, John, Paul, James, Peter, and Jude. These were all men who held the highest standards of ethics and were willing to die for their beliefs, as most of them did.

Third, these writers were credible as indicated by (1) their tendency to doubt whether Jesus rose from the dead (Matthew 28:17; Mark 16:3; Luke 24:11; John 20:24–29); (2) the inclusion of material that reflected badly on themselves (see Matthew 16:23; Mark 14:47); (3) the multiple accounts (Matthew, Mark, Luke, John, Paul, etc.) that establish their words by two or three witnesses as the court required (Deuteronomy 17:6); (4) the divergence in accounts that reveals they were not in collusion (see Matthew 28:5 cf. John 20:12); (5) confirmation of the accounts through hundreds of archaeological finds;[9] and (6) the evidence for early dates for the basic material about Jesus' death and resurrection by A.D. 55–60. Noted historian Colin Hemer confirmed that Luke wrote Acts by A.D. 62.[10] But Luke wrote the gospel of Luke, which says the same basic things about Jesus that

Matthew and Mark say, before he wrote Acts (say, by A.D. 60). Further, Bible critics admit that Paul wrote 1 Corinthians 15:1–6, which tells of the death and resurrection of Jesus, by about A.D. 55. This was only twenty-two years after Jesus' death, while more than 250 witnesses of his resurrection were still alive (see 15:6).

WHY DOES THE JESUS SEMINAR REJECT THE RELIABILITY OF THE NEW TESTAMENT WITNESSES?

Through its wrong premises and conclusions, this self-appointed group of more than seventy scholars has made outlandish claims regarding the New Testament, casting doubt on 82 percent of the teachings the Gospels ascribe to Jesus. Cofounder John Dominic Crossan went so far in his denial of the resurrection as to claim that Jesus was buried in a shallow grave, dug up by dogs, and eaten.[11] The Jesus Seminar's claims are without foundation for many reasons.

They have the wrong motive. By their own admission, the Jesus Seminar's goal is to create a new "fictive" Jesus,[12] which involves deconstructing the old picture of Jesus in the Gospels and reconstructing one that fits modern man. In view of this, no one should look to their work for the real Jesus. Their work is tainted by their confessed publicity-seeking. In their own words, "We are going to carry out our work in full public view; we will not only honor the freedom of information, we will insist on the public disclosure of our work."[13] In a frank confession, they also acknowledged the radical nature of their work. Jesus Seminar cofounder Robert Funk said, "We are probing what is most sacred to millions, and hence we will constantly border on blasphemy."[14]

They use the wrong procedure and the wrong books. The Jesus Seminar's procedure is prejudiced, attempting to determine truth by majority vote. This method is no better today than when most people believed the world was flat. The Jesus Seminar's voting is based in part on a hypothetical Gospel of Q (from German *Quelle,* meaning source) and a second-century Gospel of Thomas, which comes from Gnostic heretics. In addition, they appeal to a nonexistent *Secret Mark*. The result is that the apocryphal Gospel of Thomas is given more credibility than Mark or John.

They make the wrong assumptions. The Jesus Seminar's conclusions are based on radical presuppositions, one of which is their rejection of miracles. But if God exists, miracles are possible. Hence, any rejection of miracles is a rejection of the existence of God. What's more, their conclusions are based on the unfounded assumption that Christianity was influenced by the mystery religions. Edwin Yamauchi, noted ancient history scholar, has demonstrated that this is not the case, since the monotheistic Jewish writers of Scripture would not be using polytheistic pagan sources and could not be dependent on sources that were later than their time.[15]

They use the wrong dates. The Jesus Seminar posits unjustified late dates for the four Gospels (probably A.D. 70 to 100). By doing so they believe they are able to conclude that the New Testament is made up of later myths about Jesus. But this is contrary to the manuscript evidence that provides a copy of fragments of John from the early second century in Egypt and would argue for its Asian original in the first century. Further, the New Testament Gospels are cited in other first-century works, including *The Epistle of Barnabas, The Didache,* Clement's *Corinthians,* and Ignatius's *Seven Epistles.* Furthermore, historian Colin Hemer has demonstrated that the Gospel of Luke was written before Acts (cf. Luke 1:1 and Acts 1:1) and can be dated by strong evidence to before A.D. 60–62, during the same generation in which Jesus died.[16] In addition, even critical scholars accept that 1 Corinthians was written about A.D. 55–56, placing it within twenty-two or twenty-three years of the time Jesus died (in A.D. 33). But substantial myths would not have developed in this short amount of time while the eyewitnesses were alive to correct the error. Finally, some critical scholars are willing to admit early dates for the New Testament Gospels. The late Bishop John A. T. Robinson argued in his book *Redating the New Testament* that they were written between A.D. 40 and 60-plus.[17] This would place the first written records as close as seven years after Jesus died!

They come to the wrong conclusions. In the wake of destroying the basis for the real Jesus of the Gospels, the Jesus Seminar has no real agreement as to who Jesus actually was: a cynic, a sage, a Jewish reformer, a feminist, a prophet-teacher, a radical social prophet, or an eschatological prophet. Little wonder that something done by a group using the wrong procedure, based on the wrong books, grounded in the wrong assumptions, and employing the wrong dates would come to wrong conclusions.

Those interested in viewing the evidence for the authenticity of the four Gospels can look to such sources as Craig Blomberg's *The Historical Reliability of the Gospels*[18] and Gary Habermas's *The Historical Jesus.*[19] Better yet, pick up the four Gospels and read them afresh.

WOULD THE NEW TESTAMENT WITNESSES HAVE STOOD UP IN A COURT OF LAW?

Simon Greenleaf, one of history's greatest legal minds, former Harvard law professor, and author of a book on legal evidence,[20] carefully applied the rules of legal evidence to the Gospel accounts in his book *The Testimony of the Evangelists.* He argued that if the Gospels were submitted to the scrutiny of a court of law, "then it is believed that every honest and impartial man will act consistently with that result, by receiving their testimony in all the extent of its import."[21] He added, "Let the witnesses be compared with themselves, with each other, and with surrounding facts and circumstances; and let their testimony be sifted, as if it were given in a court of justice, on the side of the adverse party, the witness being subjected to rigorous cross-examination. The result, it is confidently believed, will be an undoubting conviction of their integrity, ability, and truth."[22]

ARE THE COPIES OF THE BIBLE RELIABLE?

The biblical scribes were meticulous in how they copied Scripture. The overall reliability has been measured in several ways. First, with regard to any major doctrine in the Bible, there has been no loss whatsoever. Every important truth of Scripture from the original text has been preserved intact in the Old Testament Hebrew and the New Testament Greek manuscripts.

Second, errors that exist in the copies are in minor matters, such as numbers that affect no major or minor doctrinal matter in the Bible (see

"Are There Errors in Bible Manuscripts and Translations," page 120). In fact, in most of these, we know either from the common sense of the text, the context, or other passages which ones are correct.

Third, not only is 100 percent of all the major truth and the vast majority of minor truth of Scripture preserved in the manuscripts we have (and in the translations based on them), but more than 99 percent of the original text can be reconstructed from the manuscripts we possess. The reason is twofold: (1) we have thousands of manuscripts, and (2) we have early manuscripts. The proximity to the original text and the multiplicity of the manuscripts enable textual scholars to accurately reconstruct the original text with more than 99 percent accuracy. Renowned Greek scholar Sir Frederic Kenyon affirmed that all manuscripts agree on the essential correctness of 99 percent of the verses in the New Testament. Another noted Greek scholar, A. T. Robertson, said the real concerns of textual criticism is on "a thousandth part of the entire text"[23] (making the New Testament 99.9 percent pure).

Conclusion

The Bible both claims and proves to be the Word of God. Both the internal and external evidence overwhelmingly reveal the accuracy and, as we'll see in the next chapter, the uniqueness of the Scriptures. Having examined its origin, nature, and reliability, we may confidently assert that the Scriptures came from God through men of God who recorded it in the Word of God.

QUESTIONS FOR REFLECTION AND DISCUSSION

1. Did God *dictate* what he wanted to communicate to the biblical authors? If not, describe how someone can hold to both biblical inerrancy and the unique human role in authorship.

2. Discuss what is meant by the assertion "The Bible *is* the Word of God." How does this differ from the statement "The Bible *contains* the Word of God"?

3. How would you respond to someone who suggests that the Bible is not historically reliable? What evidence for its credibility can you offer?

Part 2

Questions about Other Faiths

Tough Questions about the Bible, False Prophets, and the Holy Books of Other Religions

Norman Geisler

The Bible both claims and proves to be the Word of God. That is, Scripture not only declares itself to be the authoritative Word of God but also proves itself to be this very Word by overwhelming internal and external evidence. However, other books also claim to be divine revelations from God. So then, the questions before us are "Is the Bible unique?" and "Do other revelations prove to be divine as well?" I will seek to persuade that the only book that both claims and proves to be the Word of God is the Bible.

Questions about the Confirmation of Scripture as the Word of God

Many skeptics rightfully ask for the evidence that the Bible is what it claims to be—the Word of God.[1] After all, there are many books besides the

Bible that claim to come from God. Among them are these two: the Qur'an of Islam and The Book of Mormon of the Church of Jesus Christ of Latter-Day Saints. How do we know the Bible is the Word of God and they are not? Why can't they all be from God?

WHAT EVIDENCE IS THERE THAT THE BIBLE IS INSPIRED BY GOD AS IT CLAIMS TO BE?

Unlike other holy books, the Bible alone has been supernaturally confirmed to be the Word of God. For only the Scriptures were written by prophets who were supernaturally confirmed by signs and wonders. When Moses questioned how his message would be accepted, God performed miracles through him "that [the Israelites] may believe that the LORD, the God of their fathers—the God of Abraham, the God of Isaac and the God of Jacob—has appeared to you" (Exodus 4:5). Later, when Korah rose up to challenge Moses, God again miraculously intervened to vindicate his prophet (see Numbers 16)—and so, too, Elijah was confirmed to be a prophet of God by supernatural intervention on Mount Carmel (see 1 Kings 18).

In the Gospels, the Jewish teacher Nicodemus said to Jesus, "Rabbi, we know you are a teacher who has come from God. For no one could perform the miraculous signs you are doing if God were not with him" (John 3:2 see Luke 7:22). Peter declared, "Jesus of Nazareth was a man accredited by God to you by miracles, wonders and signs, which God did among you through him" (Acts 2:22). The writer of Hebrews affirms that "God also testified to [salvation through Jesus Christ] by signs, wonders and various miracles, and gifts of the Holy Spirit distributed according to his will" (Hebrews 2:4). And the apostle Paul proved his apostleship by affirming, "The things that mark an apostle—signs, wonders and miracles—were done among you with great perseverance" (2 Corinthians 12:12).

No other book in the world has authors who were confirmed in this miraculous manner. Of all the world religious leaders, neither Confucius nor Buddha nor Muhammad nor Joseph Smith was confirmed by miracles verified by contemporary and credible witnesses. The Bible alone proves to be the Word of God written by prophets and apostles of God who were confirmed by special miraculous acts of God.

IS THERE ANY OTHER EVIDENCE THAT THE BIBLE IS GOD'S WORD?

There are many lines of evidence that the Bible is God's Word,[2] but one of the most important evidences of the Bible's supernatural nature is its ability to make clear, repeated predictions about the distant future. The Old Testament has nearly two hundred predictions about the coming of Christ that were made hundreds of years in advance. Just a small sampling shows that they predicted with complete accuracy that the Messiah would be born

- of a woman (Genesis 3:15).
- of the line of Abraham (Genesis 12:1–3; 22:18).
- through the tribe of Judah (Genesis 49:10).
- as a son of David (2 Samuel 7:12–13).
- in the city of Bethlehem (Micah 5:2).
- of a virgin (Isaiah 7:14).
- and suffer and die for our sins (Isaiah 53) at about A.D. 33 (Daniel 9:24–26).[3]
- and rise from the dead (Psalm 16:11 see Psalm 2:7–8).

Even Bible critics admit all these prophecies were given two hundred to several hundred years before the time of Christ, which eliminates any guessing or reading the trends of the times. Further, these prophecies are both detailed and specific. They give the very ancestry (David), place (Bethlehem), and times (Daniel 9) of Christ's coming. No other religious book offers anything that can compare with these supernatural predictions.

HAVEN'T PSYCHICS MADE SUCCESSFUL PREDICTIONS LIKE THOSE FOUND IN THE BIBLE?

There is a quantum leap between fallible human prognosticators and the unerring prophets of Scripture. Indeed, one of the tests of false prophets was whether they ever uttered predictions that did not come to pass (Deuteronomy 18:22). Those whose prophecies failed were stoned (verse 20)—a practice that no doubt gave serious pause to any who were not absolutely sure their message was from God! Amid hundreds of prophecies, biblical prophets are not known to have made a single error.

By comparison, a study made of top psychics revealed that they were wrong 92 percent of the time.[4] Jeane Dixon, for example, was wrong the vast majority of the time. Indeed, even her biographer, Ruth Montgomery, admits that Dixon made false prophecies. "She predicted that Red China would plunge the world into war over Quemoy and Matsu in October of 1958; she thought that labor leader Walter Reuther would actively seek the presidency in 1964."[5] On October 19, 1968, Dixon assured us that Jacqueline Kennedy was not considering marriage; the next day Mrs. Kennedy wed Aristotle Onassis. She also said that World War III would begin in 1954, the Vietnam War would end in 1966, and Castro would be banished from Cuba in 1970.

A study of prophecies made by psychics in 1975 and observed until 1981, including Dixon's projections, showed that of the seventy-two predictions, only six were fulfilled in any way. Two of these were vague and two others were hardly surprising—the United States and Russia would remain leading powers and there would be no world wars. An accuracy rate around 8 percent could easily be explained by chance and a general knowledge of circumstances.

DIDN'T NOSTRADAMUS MAKE SUPER-NATURAL PREDICTIONS?

No. The highly reputed "predictions" of Nostradamus were not so amazing at all.[6] Consider one of the more famous ones:

The alleged California earthquake. Nostradamus is alleged to have predicted a great earthquake in California for May 10, 1981—a prediction reported on May 6, 1981, in *USA Today.* However, no such quake occurred. As a matter of fact, Nostradamus mentioned no country, city, or year. He spoke only of a "rumbling earth" in a "new city" and a "very mighty quake" on May 10. Considering the thousands of earthquakes that take place, an occurrence this general was bound to take place somewhere and sometime.

DO NOSTRADAMUS'S PREDICTIONS FAIL THE TEST OF A TRUE PROPHET?

Nostradamus's forecasts are far from supernatural. They are general, vague, and explainable on purely natural grounds.

False prophecies. One of the clear signs of false prophets is that they make false prophecies (see "What Are the Tests for a False Prophet? (page 136). If Nostradamus's predictions are taken literally, then many are false. If they are not, then they can mean many things and fit different "fulfillments." As apologetics expert John Ankerberg put it, "It is an undeniable fact that Nostradamus gave numerous false prophecies."[7]

Vague predictions. The vast majority of Nostradamus's prognostications are so ambiguous and vague that they can have many different fulfillments. Consider this one: "Scythe by the Pond, in conjunction with Sagittarius at the high point of its ascendant—disease, famine, death by soldiery—the century/age draws near its renewal" (Century I, verse 6). The possible interpretations are legion. The prediction can be understood in many ways with a wide possibility that something in the future will fit it and make it appear, in retrospect, to be supernatural.

Predictions understood only after the fact. Even Nostradamus himself acknowledged that his predictions were written in such a manner that "they could not possibly be understood until they were interpreted after the event and by it."[8] But there is nothing miraculous or supernatural about reading a fulfillment back into a prophecy that could not be clearly seen there before the alleged fulfillment. Not a single prediction of Nostradamus has ever proved genuine, indicating either he was a false prophet or he wasn't seriously claiming to be making real predictions.

Confessed occult and demonic sources. Nostradamus admitted demonic inspiration when he wrote, "The tenth of the Calends of April roused by evil persons; the light extinguished; diabolical assembly searching for the bones of the devil (*damant*—demon) according to Psellos."[9] Andre Lamont, author of *Nostradamus Sees All,* made this observation: "The utilization of the demons or black angels are recommended by ancient writers on magic. They claim that they have much knowledge of temporal matters and, once under control, will give much information to the operator." He added, "Nostradamus could not have avoided such a temptation."[10]

WHAT ARE THE TESTS FOR A FALSE PROPHET?

The Bible lists many tests for a false prophet. In the passages below I've numbered some of these tests.

In the book of Deuteronomy Moses declares this:

> If a prophet, or one who foretells by dreams, appears among you and announces to you a miraculous sign or wonder, and if the sign or wonder of which he has spoken takes place, and he says, [1] "Let us follow other gods" (gods you have not known) "and let us worship them," you must not listen to the words of that prophet or dreamer.
>
> *Deuteronomy 13:1–3*

> Let no one be found among you who [2] sacrifices his son or daughter in the fire, who [3] practices divination or [4] sorcery, [5] interprets omens, engages in [6] witchcraft, or [7] casts spells, or who is a [8] medium or [9] spiritist or who [10] consults the dead. . . .
>
> But a prophet who presumes to speak in my name anything I have not commanded him to say, or a prophet [11] who speaks in the name of other gods, must be put to death.
>
> You may say to yourselves, "How can we know when a message has not been spoken by the LORD?" [12] If what a prophet proclaims in the name of the LORD does not take place or come true, that is a message the LORD has not spoken. That prophet has spoken presumptuously.
>
> *Deuteronomy 18:10–11, 20–22*

The Bible also condemns those who use [13] astrology (Exodus 22:18; Leviticus 19:26, 31; 20:6; Jeremiah 27:9; Ezekiel 13:7, 18).

In the New Testament, Paul added to the list by writing the following to Timothy:

> The Spirit clearly says that in later times some will [14] abandon the faith and follow [15] deceiving spirits and things taught by demons. Such teachings come through [16] hypocritical liars, whose consciences have been seared as with a hot iron. They [17] forbid people to marry and [18] order them to abstain from certain foods.
>
> *1 Timothy 4:1–3*

Paul used another test when he said, [19] "But even if we or an angel from heaven should preach a gospel other than the one we preached to you, let him be eternally condemned!" (Galatians 1:8).

Finally, we have this from John:

> Dear friends, do not believe every spirit, but test the spirits to see whether they are from God, because many false prophets have gone out into the world. [20] This is how you can recognize the Spirit of God: Every spirit that acknowledges that Jesus Christ has come in the flesh is from God, but every spirit that does not acknowledge Jesus is not from God.
>
> *1 John 4:1–3*

DID THE BIBLICAL AUTHORS MEASURE UP TO THESE TESTS?

The biblical authors did indeed measure up. In fact, they were the ones who laid down the tests listed above. One of the clearest and most definitive tests was the ability to perform miracles in support of their claims. Moses performed miracles to confirm he was of God (Exodus 4–12). The apostles also did many miracles (Matthew 10:1–8), as did Jesus (John 3:2; 20:30; Hebrews 2:3–4). Paul used miracles as proof that he was an apostle of God, saying, "The things that mark an apostle—signs, wonders and miracles—were done among you with great perseverance" (2 Corinthians 12:12).

WHY CAN'T THE HOLY BOOKS OF OTHER RELIGIONS ALSO BE FROM GOD?

In our multicultural, pluralistic society, people often claim that all religions are true. "Why assume," they ask, "that the holy book of just one religion is from God? Why can't they all represent truth?" Because they teach contradictory things, and contradictions cannot all be true. For example, if George Washington was the first president of the United States of America, then it cannot also be true that Thomas Jefferson was the first president.

Likewise, if the Bible declares that Jesus died on the cross and rose bodily from the dead three days later (see 1 Corinthians 15:1–6), and the Qur'an teaches that he did not (see Sura 4:157), both books cannot be true on such a crucial teaching. One of them has to be wrong. Further, if the writings of Joseph Smith teach that there are many gods (polytheism), which they do,[11] and the Bible declares that there is only one God, as it does (see Deuteronomy 6:4; 1 Corinthians 8:4), then both of these writings cannot be true. If the Bible is true, Smith is wrong; if Smith is right, the Bible is wrong. Of course, there are some truths in these other holy books that do not contradict the Bible, but what does contradict the Bible cannot be true.

ISN'T IT NARROW-MINDED TO CLAIM THAT ONLY ONE RELIGION HAS THE TRUTH?

Christianity does not claim that there is no truth in non-Christian religious books. It only claims that the Bible is true and that whatever is contradictory to the Bible is false. There is much that is good and true in non-Christian religions. For example, Confucius said, "Do not do to others what you would not have them do to you"—sometimes called the negative Golden Rule. This is not contradictory to the positive Golden Rule of Jesus: "Do to others what you would have them do to you, for this sums up the Law and the Prophets" (Matthew 7:12). Also, Buddhism and most other religions are in harmony with Christianity in teaching that we should respect our parents and that murder is wrong. Christianity does not teach that only the Bible contains truth. It only affirms that the Bible is true and that everything that contradicts it is false, since contradictions cannot both be true.

Questions about the Extent of Scripture

Bible critics and skeptics often ask about the so-called "missing books of the Bible." Is the Bible complete?[12] Have parts of it been lost? If so, were they important parts? This is the question of the canon (rule) of the Bible, that is, which books belong in the Bible and should be used as the measuring rod of truth?

IS THE OLD TESTAMENT COMPLETE?

The completeness of the Old Testament is confirmed by several facts. These include the testimony of Judaism, the testimony of Christ, and the testimony of the Christian church (see the following questions).

WHAT IS THE TESTIMONY OF JUDAISM ABOUT THE COMPLETENESS OF THE OLD TESTAMENT?

The Old Testament is the Jewish Scriptures. It was written by Jews and for Jews, and Jewish scholars have unanimously acknowledged that the twenty-four books are identical to the thirty-nine books in the Protestant Old Testament but numbered differently. That these books comprised the complete Jewish canon is based on several considerations.

First, the very fact that the books are combined in certain ways to make twenty-four (or twenty-two) reveals that they are considered to be complete, since this is the number of letters in the complete Hebrew alphabet (there being two double letters, making the alternate of twenty-two or twenty-four). In order to make the thirty-nine books listed in our Old Testament come out to twenty-four (the number in today's Jewish Bible), they classed all twelve minor prophets as one book and combined all the first and second books (1 and 2 Samuel, 1 and 2 Kings, 1 and 2 Chronicles, and Ezra-Nehemiah) to make one book for each pair. Some Jewish sources (like

Josephus) renumber them to twenty-two (the exact number of the root Hebrew alphabet). This numbering of books indicates their belief that their canon was complete.

Furthermore, there are explicit statements in Judaism affirming the closure of their canon. Josephus said that "from Artaxerxes [Malachi's day, about 400 B.C.] until our time everything has been recorded, but has not been deemed worthy of like credit with what preceded, because the exact successions of the prophets ceased." The Jewish Talmud adds, "After the latter prophets Haggai, Zechariah, and Malachi, the Holy Spirit departed from Israel."[13]

Finally, Jewish scholars, such as Philo and Josephus, those from Jamnia (the Jewish city of scholars from A.D. 70–132), and the Talmud all agree on the number of books in their canon. No branch of Judaism has ever accepted any other books or rejected any of the thirty-nine (twenty-four) books of the Protestant Old Testament. The Jewish canon is considered closed, and it has exactly the same books as the evangelical Old Testament canon.

WHAT DID JESUS SAY ABOUT THE COMPLETENESS OF THE OLD TESTAMENT?

Jesus confirmed the closure of the Old Testament canon in several ways. In his numerous use of the Old Testament Scriptures, he never cited any book other than one of the twenty-four (thirty-nine) canonical books of the Jewish Old Testament. What's more, he cited from every major section of the Old Testament—both Law and Prophets, as well as the later division of the Prophets known as "Writings." But he never quoted any books known as the Apocrypha. Further, Jesus in Matthew 23:35 defined the limits of the Old Testament canon as ending in 2 Chronicles (the book listed last in the Jewish Old Testament) by the phrase "from the blood of righteous Abel [Genesis 4] to the blood of Zechariah [2 Chronicles 24:20–22]." The phrase was a Jewish equivalent of the Christian phrase "from Genesis to Revelation," indicating a complete Jewish canon of Scripture. Furthermore, phrases like "Law or the Prophets" (Matthew 5:17) and "Moses and all the Prophets" (Luke 24:27) are used by Jesus to indicate the complete canon of Jewish

Scripture. Indeed, Jesus used the phrase in parallel with the phrase "all the Scriptures" (Luke 24:27). Being a faithful Jew, Jesus, who came "not to abolish the Law or the Prophets" (Matthew 5:17), accepted the same closed Jewish canon as did Judaism, which has always been the same books as the thirty-nine books of the Protestant Old Testament.

WHAT DID EARLY CHRISTIANS SAY ABOUT THE COMPLETENESS OF THE OLD TESTAMENT?

Early Christians manifested their acceptance of the Jewish canon in several ways. First, they quoted from these books as Scripture. With the exception of the heretical teacher Origen, the consensus of the church fathers of the first four centuries supported the books in the Jewish Old Testament and no more.[14]

When the Apocryphal books were cited, they were not given the divine authority accorded the thirty-nine canonical books. Rather, they were used in a manner similar to that of Paul's use of noninspired Greek thinkers—e.g., Acts 17:28; 1 Corinthians 15:33; Titus 1:12; or the Pseudepigrapha (false writings; e.g., Jude 9, 14)—cited for some truth in them but not as inspired. Even Augustine, whose influence led many after him to accept the Old Testament Apocrypha, recognized that these books were not in the Jewish canon.

Most of the alleged citations of the Apocrypha by other early writers do not really support the inspiration of these extracanonical books. Noted canonical scholar Roger Beckwith makes this observation:

> When one examines the passages in the early Fathers which are supposed to establish the canonicity of the Apocrypha, one finds that some of them are taken from the alternative Greek text of Ezra (1 Esdras) or from additions of appendices to Daniel, Jeremiah, or some other canonical book, which . . . are really not relevant; that others of them are not quotations from the Apocrypha at all; and that, of those which are, many do not give any indication that the book is regarded as Scripture.[15]

DID THE ROMAN CATHOLIC CHURCH ADD BOOKS TO THE JEWISH OLD TESTAMENT?

Yes. These books, known as the Apocrypha, were written between 250 B.C. and 150 A.D. They were written by Jews about Jewish history and beliefs in the intertestamental times, but they did not claim to be inspired, nor did Judaism ever accept them as inspired. Nevertheless, Roman Catholic officials added eleven of these apocryphal books to the Bible by an alleged infallible proclamation of the Council of Trent (A.D. 1546).

This adding of apocryphal books is rejected by Protestants because

- these books do not claim to be inspired.
- they were not written by prophets.
- they were not confirmed by miracles.
- they contain no new supernatural prophecies.
- they contain false teachings and errors.
- they were never accepted by Judaism as inspired.
- they are never quoted as Scripture in the New Testament.
- Jesus accepted and confirmed the Jewish canon, which was called the Law and the Prophets (Matthew 5:17–18; Luke 24:27).
- they were rejected by most major church fathers in the early church, including the great Roman Catholic biblical scholar Jerome.
- the grounds on which Roman Catholics accepted them was faulty—claiming Christian usage rather than their being written by a prophet or apostle as the reason (see John 14:26; 16:13; Ephesians 2:20; Hebrews 1:1; 2:3–4).[16]

HOW DO WE KNOW THE NEW TESTAMENT IS COMPLETE?

The New Testament was written between about A.D. 50 and 90. Several lines of evidence support the evangelical belief that the New Testament canon is closed. Jesus promised a closed canon by limiting the teaching authority to the apostles, who all died before the end of the first century.[17]

WHAT DID JESUS PROMISE ABOUT THE FORMATION OF THE NEW TESTAMENT?

The New Testament gives clear indications that Jesus' revelation to the apostles would complete the biblical revelation. Jesus was the full and complete revelation of the Old Testament. In the Sermon on the Mount he said of the whole Old Testament, "Do not think that I have come to abolish the Law or the Prophets; I have not come to abolish [the Law and the Prophets] but to fulfill them" (Matthew 5:17). Indeed, the book of Hebrews teaches that Jesus is the full and final revelation of God in "the last days." The author of Hebrews wrote this:

> In the past God spoke to our forefathers through the prophets at many times and in various ways, but in these last days he has spoken to us by his Son, whom he appointed heir of all things, and through whom he made the universe. The Son is the radiance of God's glory and the exact representation of his being.
>
> *Hebrews 1:1–3*

Further, the author of Hebrews refers to Jesus as "superior to" the angels (1:4), a "better hope" than the law (7:19), and "better" than the Old Testament law and priesthood (9:23). Indeed, his revelation and redemption is said to be eternal (5:9; 9:12, 15) and once for all (9:28; 10:12–14). So Jesus was the full and final revelation of God to humankind. He alone could say, "Anyone who has seen me has seen the Father" (John 14:9). And of Jesus Christ alone could it be said that "in [him] all the fullness of the Deity lives in bodily form" (Colossians 2:9).

WHAT DID JESUS' APOSTLES SAY ABOUT THE NEW TESTAMENT?

Jesus chose, commissioned, and credentialed twelve apostles (cf. Hebrews 2:3–4) to teach this full and final revelation he gave them (Matthew 10:1). And before Jesus left this world he promised to guide these apostles into all truth, saying, "The Holy Spirit . . . will teach you all things and will remind you of everything I have said to you" (John 14:26). And, "When he, the Spirit of truth, comes, he will guide you into all truth" (John 16:13). This is why the church is said to be "built on the foundation of the apostles and prophets" (Ephesians 2:20) and at its beginning the church "devoted themselves to the apostles' teaching" (Acts 2:42). If the apostles of Jesus did not teach this completed revelation of God, then Jesus was wrong. But as the Son of God he could not be wrong in what he taught. Therefore, the full and final revelation of God in Jesus Christ was given by the apostles.

The apostles of Jesus lived and died in the first century. So the record of this full and final revelation of Jesus to the apostles was completed in the first century. Indeed, one of the qualifications of an apostle was that he was an eyewitness of the resurrection of Jesus, which occurred in the first century (see Acts 1:22). Anyone who lived after that time was a "false apostle" (2 Corinthians 11:13). When Paul's credentials as an apostle were challenged, he replied, "Am I not an apostle? Have I not seen Jesus our Lord?" (1 Corinthians 9:1). Indeed, he is listed with the other apostles as the last to have seen the resurrected Christ (see 1 Corinthians 15:6–8).

WHAT EVIDENCE DID THE APOSTLES SHOW FOR THEIR AUTHORITY?

So that there would be no doubt as to who was authorized to teach this full and final revelation of God in Jesus Christ, God gave to the apostles the ability to do works of a supernatural origin and power, who in turn imparted this gift and power to their associates (see Acts 6:6; 8:15–19; 2 Timothy 1:6). That these "signs, wonders and miracles" were unique to the apostles is clear from the fact that they were called "the things that mark an apostle" (2 Corinthians 12:12) and that certain things could only occur through the "laying on of the apostles' hands" (Acts 8:18; cf. 19:6). Further, this "power" was promised to the apostles (Acts 1:8), and after Jesus went to the Father (cf. John 14:12), they exercised or gave special apostolic functions and powers, including striking people dead who lied to the Holy Spirit (see Acts 5:9–11) and performing special signs and wonders (see Acts 5:12; 2 Corinthians 12:12; Hebrews 2:3–4), which included even raising the dead on command (see Matthew 10:8; Acts 20:7–12).

Finally, there is only one authentic record of apostolic teaching in existence—the twenty-seven books of the New Testament. All other books that claim inspiration come from the second century or later. These books are known as the New Testament Apocrypha and are clearly not written by apostles, since the apostles all died before the end of the first century.

Since we know that the twenty-seven books of the New Testament have been copied accurately from the very beginning (see "Are the Copies of the Bible Reliable," page 126), the only remaining question is whether *all* of the apostolic writings from the first century have been preserved. If they have, then these twenty-seven books complete the canon of Scripture. And anything written after them cannot be a revelation of God to the church.

WERE ALL THE APOSTOLIC AND PROPHETIC WRITINGS PRESERVED IN THE NEW TESTAMENT?

Yes, we have every reason to believe they were. There are two lines of evidence that all the inspired writings of the apostles and their associates were preserved and are found in the twenty-seven books of the New Testament. The first reason is based on the character of God and the second on the care exercised by the church.

HOW DOES THE CHARACTER OF GOD GUARANTEE THE COMPLETENESS OF THE NEW TESTAMENT?

Since the God of the Bible is all-knowing (Psalm 139:1–6; 147:5), all-good (Psalm 136; 1 Peter 2:3), and all-powerful (Genesis 1:1; Matthew 19:26), it follows that he would not inspire books for the faith and practice of believers down through the centuries and then fail to preserve them. Lost inspired books would be a lapse in God's providence. The God who cares for the sparrows will certainly care for his Scriptures. And the God who has preserved his general revelation in nature (Romans 1:19–20) will certainly not fail to preserve his special revelation in Scripture (Romans

3:2). In short, if God inspired them (2 Timothy 3:16), God will preserve them. God completes what God begins (Philippians 1:6).

DID THE CHURCH CAREFULLY PRESERVE THE WHOLE NEW TESTAMENT?

The church has preserved the whole New Testament. Not only does God's providence promise the preservation of all inspired books, the preservation of these books by the church also confirms it—a preservation manifested in several ways.

First, a collection of these books was made from the earliest times. Even within the New Testament itself this preservation process was put into action. Luke refers to other written records (Luke 1:1–4)—possibly Matthew and Mark. In Paul's first letter to Timothy (5:18), he quotes the Gospel of Luke (10:7). Peter refers to a collection of Paul's letters (2 Peter 3:15–16). Paul charged that his letter of 1 Thessalonians be read "to all the brothers" (5:27). And he commanded the church at Colosse, "After this letter has been read to you, see that it is also read in the church of the Laodiceans" (Colossians 4:16). Jude (verses 6–7) apparently had access to Peter's second letter (2 Peter 2:4–6). And John's book of Revelation was circulated to the churches of Asia Minor (Revelation 1:4). So the apostolic church itself was involved by divine imperative in the preservation of the apostolic writings.

Second, the contemporaries of the apostles showed an awareness of their mentors' writings, quoting from them prolifically. Following them, the church fathers of the second to fourth centuries made some 36,289 citations from the New Testament, including every verse except for eleven of them! This included 19,368 citations from the Gospels, 1,352 from Acts, 14,035 from Paul's Epistles, 870 from the General Epistles, and 664 from Revelation.[18] The church fathers of the second century alone cited from every major book of the New Testament and all but one minor one (3 John, which they simply may have had no occasion to cite). This reveals not only their great respect for the writings of the apostles but also their ardent desire to preserve their written words.

Third, when challenged by heretical teaching, such as that of Marcion the Gnostic, who rejected all of the New Testament except part of Luke and ten of Paul's letters (accepting all but 1 and 2 Timothy and Titus), the church responded by officially defining the extent of the canon. Lists of apostolic books and collections of the apostles' writings were made from early times, beginning with the second century. These include the Muratorian (A.D. 170), Apostolic (ca. A.D. 300), Cheltenham (ca. A.D. 360), and Athanasian (A.D. 367) lists, as well as the Old Latin translation (ca. A.D. 200). This process culminated in the late fourth and early fifth centuries at the Councils of Hippo (A.D. 393) and Carthage (A.D. 410), which listed the twenty-seven books of the New Testament as the complete canon. Catholics of all kinds, Protestants, and Anglicans have accepted this as the permanent verdict of the church. Evangelical Protestants agree that the canon is closed.

IS THE WHOLE BIBLE COMPLETE?

The Bible is complete. There is no evidence that any inspired book has been lost. This is confirmed by the providence of God, the immediate and careful preservation exercised by the church, and the absence of any evidence of any other prophetic or apostolic book. Alleged contrary examples are easily explained as either noninspired works to which the biblical author made reference or inspired works contained in the sixty-six inspired books but with another name.

WHY ARE NONINSPIRED BOOKS MENTIONED IN THE BIBLE?

Sometimes a biblical author cited noninspired books. The apostle Paul cited some truths from pagan poets (Acts 17:28; Titus 1:12). Jude may have referred to some pseudepigraphal books (The Testament of Moses and the book of Enoch; see Jude 9, 14) that are rejected by both Judaism and all segments of Christianity.

Other noninspired books cited in the Old Testament include the Book of the Wars of the LORD (Numbers 21:14), the Book of Jashar (Joshua 10:13), and the book of the annals of Solomon (1 Kings 11:41). These were simply sources to which the biblical author had occasion to refer to some truth contained in them. Books in this category could even have been written by a prophet or apostle who made no pretense on that occasion to be offering a revelation from God for the people of God. After all, even authors of inspired books had occasion for normal correspondence relating to business or family. "The records of Shemaiah the prophet" (2 Chronicles 12:15) seems to fit in this slot.[19]

DO MORMONS BELIEVE THAT THE BIBLE IS INSPIRED BY GOD?

Not really. While in theory Mormons accept the inspiration of the original manuscripts of the Bible, in practice they believe that the copies are riddled with errors. *The Missionary Pal* lists a section on "Bible Errors"[20] and gives examples of "errors" in the Bible, such as the two accounts of Judas's death (Matthew 27:5; Acts 1:18) and two reports of Paul's vision (Acts 9:7; 22:9).[21] In fact, Joseph Smith made his own "inspired" translation of the Bible (the Joseph Smith Translation), which contains thousands of changes from the King James Bible.

The official statement of Mormonism about the Bible is this: "We believe the Bible to be the word of God as far as it is translated correctly; we also believe the book of Mormon to be the word of God" (eighth article of faith). But in practice Mormon leaders from Joseph Smith on have said the Bible has not been translated accurately. So it gives a wrong impression to say they believe that the Bible is the Word of God. If it is, why would God command Joseph Smith to make an "inspired translation" of the Bible that contains thousands of changes from the Bible in use in Smith's day, even omitting a whole book (Song of Songs)?

IS THERE CONFIRMATION THAT MORMON SCRIPTURES ARE FROM GOD?

None whatsoever. Unlike the Gospels, the witnesses to the claims of The Book of Mormon were not supported by supernatural events, as Jesus and the apostles were (see "What Evidence Is There That the Bible Is Inspired by God as It Claims to Be?" page 132). Further, later Mormon writings contradict earlier ones.[22] What's more, Joseph Smith fits the tests for a false prophet (see "What Are the Tests for a False Prophet?" page 136), since he used means of divination and made false prophecies. In addition, neither Joseph Smith nor his witnesses were confirmed by such miracles as healing the blind, lame and deaf, and raising the dead (cf. Matthew 10:8; Luke 7:21–22). Finally, the witnesses of The Book of Mormon were not credible.

ARE THERE EVIDENCES THAT THE BOOK OF MORMON IS INSPIRED?

Mormons offer the eleven witnesses to The Book of Mormon as proof of its divine origin. But their testimony lacks credibility for many reasons. First, even if the alleged witnesses did see some kind of plates of The Book of Mormon, it does not mean that what was written on them was true. Second, even if some of the witnesses believed they saw some angel-like beings, it does not mean they were not hallucinating. Third, even if they actually saw some angels, it does not mean that they were good angels (the devil transformed into an angel of light—2 Corinthians 11:14). Fourth, the "gospel" of works the angel revealed to Smith was contrary to the gospel of grace preached by Paul, who said, "Even if we or an angel from heaven should preach a gospel other than the one we preached to you, let him be eternally condemned!" (Galatians 1:8). Fifth, the eleven witnesses to The Book of Mormon could not read what was on the plates, so they couldn't even vouch for the content of the message on the plates. Sixth, in another case in which Joseph Smith claimed to be able to translate the Book of Abraham, the manuscript was later discovered, translated by competent scholars from Egypt, and proved to be a total fraud having nothing to do with Abraham. Rather, it was an Egyptian "Book of Breathings." Why, then, should The Book of Mormon be considered anything else? Seventh, there is a serious question about the credibility of the witnesses themselves even seeing what they claimed to have seen.

IS THE QUR'AN THE WORD OF GOD?

Muslims assert that the Qur'an itself claims to come from God through the prophet Muhammad (cf. Sura 39:1–2). The great Sunni authority Abu Hanifa expressed the orthodox belief that "the Qur'an is the word of God, and is His inspired word and revelation. It is a necessary attribute of God. It is not God, but still is inseparable from God." Of course, "It is written in a volume, it is read in a language, . . . but God's word is uncreated."[23]

Nevertheless, the Qur'an lacks any real evidence that it is the Word of God. Consider just a few crucial points. First, Muhammad himself first believed the message he got from an angel choking him was a demon. Muslim biographer M. H. Haykal wrote vividly of Muhammad's plaguing fear that he was demon-possessed: "Stricken with panic, Muhammad arose and asked himself, 'What did I see? Did possession of the devil which I feared all along come to pass?' Muhammad looked to his right and his left but saw nothing. For a while he stood there trembling with fear and stricken with awe. He feared the cave might be haunted and that he might run away still unable to explain what he saw."[24]

Second, the Qur'an contradicts the Bible on essential teachings. We have already seen that there is strong evidence that the Bible is the Word of God (see pages 132–33). And we know that contradictory truth claims cannot both be true (see page 138). For example, the Qur'an says that Jesus did not die on the cross and rise from the dead three days later (Sura 4:157–158). But this is one of the essential and often repeated truths of the Bible (cf. 1 Corinthians 15:1–19).

Third, although Muhammad recognized that prophets before him were confirmed by miracles of nature, he himself refused to perform any miracles to confirm his claims to be a prophet (Sura 3:181–84).

Fourth, unlike the Bible, the Qur'an has no specific, multiple, and long-term predictions that came to pass without fail. The best supposed example of a predictive prophecy is about the Romans avenging a defeat (Sura 30:2–4), but this is vague, indefinite, and humanly predictable.[25]

Fifth, the Qur'an contains contradictions and scientific errors. An example of a scientific error is its assertion that Adam was made out of a "blood clot" (Sura 23:14). And a contradiction is found in the fact that the Qur'an claims that there can be no change in the Words of God (Sura 10:64), which for Muslims is the Qur'an. For "there is none that can alter the Words (and Decrees) of God" (Sura 6:34). Yet the Qur'an teaches the doctrine of abrogation by which later revelations annul previous ones. Sura 2:106 speaks of "revelations . . . we abrogate or cause to be forgotten. . . ." Then it turns around and declares that "we substitute one revelation for another," admitting in the same verse that Muhammad's contemporaries called him a "forger" for doing so!

Sixth, the Qur'an teaches an inferior view of marriage (namely, polygamy) and of women. Muhammad allowed four wives for his followers (Sura 4:3) but said God made an exception for him to have more (Sura 33:50). He may have had as many as fifteen wives. As for the treatment of women, the Qur'an allowed men to "scourge [beat] them" if they even suspected them of unfaithfulness (Sura 4:34).

Conclusion

At the back of this book there is a list of excellent resources that can help you fulfill your biblical mandate to "know how to answer everyone" (Colossians 4:6) and to "be ready to give a defense to everyone" (1 Peter 3:15 NKJV). Some of these books contain a more complete list of questions and answers about the Bible.[26]

QUESTIONS FOR REFLECTION
AND DISCUSSION

1. What are some of the Bible's tests for a false prophet? How might you apply this biblical understanding to counter other beliefs about certain prophets?

2. What are some of the internal and external evidences for the completion of the biblical canon? Specifically, how did Jesus confirm the authority and finality of the Old and the New Testaments?

3. Given what you've read in this chapter, outline how you might begin to respond to a Mormon regarding the authority and reliability of The Book of Mormon versus the Bible.

Chapter 8

Tough Questions about Hinduism and Transcendental Meditation

L. T. Jeyachandran

Christians in the West face a culture that is increasingly influenced by New Age and other Eastern religious philosophies and practices. Famous personalities who have adopted iconoclastic lifestyles and belief systems—for example, Shirley MacLaine and numerous others—have added to the newfound fascination. Deepak Chopra, a medical doctor originally from India and now practicing in the United States, is advancing techniques of meditation to lower blood pressure and act as stress-busters for those living tension-filled, frenetic lifestyles. His books can be obtained in any bookstore today. *Reiki,* a Japanese New Age healing technique, suggests that the infinite energy of the universe can be focused on a tumor, and healing can take place if the right methodology is adopted. Numerous talismans claiming magical powers are now available by mail order, and columns of reputable dailies carry astrological predictions. In these next two chapters, I will deal with questions relating to Hinduism, Buddhism, and Eastern pantheistic worldviews in an attempt to cast some light on how to understand and counter these perspectives.

The purpose of this book is not only to help the reader locate errors in the worldviews that challenge the truths of the historic Christian faith but to equip the reader with an approach to share Christ with proponents of such views. In this context it is useful to identify the relationship between truth and error, between original and counterfeit.

It may be of interest to note that every error contains an element of truth. A simple example from arithmetic would be helpful to illustrate the point. For the sum $2 + 2$, the correct answer is 4. Let us call it T. There is only one correct answer, but theoretically there are an infinite number of wrong answers. If you take one of the wrong answers, say 5, you would see that, while it is wrong, it is, in a somewhat perverted sense, dependent on the right answer—it has no original existence but is derived by adding 1 to T, that is, $T + 1$. In the same way, another wrong answer, 3, is $T-1$. We could therefore say that, while the true answer is absolute, the incorrect answer is relative to the correct answer because it is arrived at by adding to or subtracting from the right answer. No wonder the Bible advises us not to add anything or take anything away from what God has revealed to us (Revelation 22:18–19)!

This is not idle theorizing. Consider two immediate implications:

1.   Error is a parasite on the truth. Our encounter with any counterfeit should therefore lead us to ask, "What is the Christian original of this counterfeit?" The answer to this question is critical, because it would throw the truth of the Christian position on that particular issue into clear relief— which would help us, in turn, to articulate our reply to the counterfeit. Truth unchallenged becomes a dogma that is held uncritically. We need to take advantage of the multitude of errors that swamps us today to relearn our faith from different perspectives and thus be strengthened in it. Paul advised his readers that his ministry was to *confirm* the gospel as well as to *defend* it (Philippians 1:7).

2.   We will also discover that the counterfeit has been arrived at by a twist of the truth at an important point. In other words, every error has an element of truth. This common element should help us build bridges to our antagonists and affirm them in whatever is true in their point of view.

Thereafter, we should be able to demonstrate (gently and respectfully—1 Peter 3:15) the vital point of departure that has resulted in the final erroneous product.

The answers to the questions posed below follow the same pattern without necessarily explicating the methodology at every step of the argument. An outline of an evangelistic response has also been given at the appropriate places so that these chapters are not seen to be simply theoretical (although that is crucial) but can be practically useful in conversational situations. At the end of this series of questions, we should emerge more robust in our faith in the uniqueness of Christ and more sensitive to those who believe otherwise.

WHY IS THERE SUCH A HIGH DEGREE OF INTEREST IN EASTERN RELIGIONS AMONG WESTERNERS?

The most memorable event that inaugurated the entry of Hindu thought into the West was the visit to the United States of Swami Vivekananda in 1893 when he took by storm the World Congress on Religions in Chicago. He began his speech with the politically correct phrase "Brothers and sisters," which was greeted by several minutes of thunderous applause. He went on to expatiate upon the essential unity of all things and beings—a fundamental part of Indian pantheism. (See the following question for an explanation of the word *pantheism*.) This approach greatly appealed to the syncretists at the conference, because it implied that everyone was acceptable to God (because every approach to God was equally truthful) and therefore all were brothers and sisters.

In his interaction with Christians at this conference, Swami Vivekananda also denied the existence of sin, because all reality was one and therefore there could be no *final* distinction between right and wrong. He is supposed to have made the memorable statement "It is sinful to call man a sinner." He substantiated his position by positing the ultimate unity of all things, including apparently conflicting beliefs.

More recently, the hippie movement of the 1960s was the watershed of Eastern religious thought in the West. It saw a number of young people, a significant number of whom were from Christian homes, wandering to the East in search of fulfillment. They understood their native Christianity to be too cerebral and incapable of meeting the intimate subjective needs of their hearts. They saw in the God of the Christians an authoritarian figure who was arbitrary and cruel. They sensed that Eastern meditation was more likely to bring them into direct contact with the transcendent. The exotic nature of the beliefs, practices, and rituals offered a welcome change from the rather colorless Christianity that had been their experience.[1]

Some of the first New Age movement gurus who arrived in the West—Maharishi Mahesh Yogi, for example—packaged Hindu beliefs and practices so that they were intellectually and socially acceptable in the West. The yogi promoted their teachings in some of the American public schools under the title "Science of Creative Intelligence." (However, in 1977, these academic departments were ruled unconstitutional in American courts for teaching religion.) Currently, people like Deepak Chopra have popularized various New Age techniques of relieving stress in the context of a society that is overly competitive, industrialized, and affluent.

Christians should not only look at the theological and philosophical answers proposed by the New Age movement but also examine the existential context in which they have taken root. In passing, we'll also see how we could address these areas from a Christian point of view. For the sake of brevity, I state them in the following paragraphs.

It is not difficult to see that the New Age movement thrives on the subjective. On the other hand, the Christian faith, particularly in order to defend itself against the onslaught of atheistic secularism and relativism of earlier periods, tended to emphasize the objective. In fact, Christian apologetics has been founded on the necessity of the objective nature of the Christian faith. In so doing, we seem to have lost touch with the subjective answers that Christianity offers to the seeker, a fact clearly brought out by the popularity of apologist Ravi Zacharias's book *Cries of the Heart*.[2]

Without abandoning the need for objectivity and historicity as characteristics of the truth, we need to unashamedly offer the subjective dimensions of the gospel—"Taste and see that the LORD is good" (Psalm 34:8). Every objective statement of truth that Jesus makes—particularly in the famous "I am" statements of the Gospel of John—are accompanied by calls to a subjective commitment and experience.

The emphasis of the subjective could often be accompanied by an "escape from reason," a phrase that formed the title of the last of Francis Schaeffer's trilogy.[3] In that prophetic book written in the early 1970s, Schaeffer could see the spread of the New Age movement in the West accompanied particularly by the abandonment of rationality. The postmodern deconstructionist movement has thus provided fertile ground for the spread of Eastern movements. (Indeed, it may be pertinent to note that from a philosophical point of view, India was "postmodern" at least twelve centuries before it started on the present road to modernity!)

Paul's epistemological note in 1 Corinthians 2:10—that true wisdom comes from an inner revelation of the Spirit—is a subject that needs to be developed as part of our apologetic. Our subjective experience of Christ is rooted in an objective historical reality of God in Christ. Only by adopting this approach consistently in our churches can we ensure that the subjective needs of people are met without giving up the tenets of rationality. Teaching about the *belief that* Christianity is true should always be accompanied by the invitation to *belief in* Christ, who alone can satisfy our subjective longings.

Atheism, which was fashionable some decades ago, left behind a fragmented approach to truth, as it lacked the unifying factor of a Creator-God. The New Age movement has filled this gap by positing the basic unity of all things in an infinite impersonal entity. *Brahman* is the term employed by the Indian pantheistic philosophy of *Advaita,* or nondualism. The Japanese healing technique of *Reiki* invokes the unity of the "infinite" energy of the universe that can be successfully manipulated by humans using various methods. Zen Buddhism advocates meditation techniques (just as pantheistic Hinduism offers transcendental meditation) to merge with the infinite consciousness of the universe. Words such as *energy* and *consciousness* litter New Age vocabulary. The underlying thrust is that fragmentation can be overcome only by rising above or transcending the diversity—hence, Transcendental Meditation (see "What Is Transcendental Meditation?" page 163)—that clutters our existence, thus allowing one to seek merger with the Infinite Reality.

The Christian answer at this point should be an equal emphasis on unity and diversity. The being of the triune God who encompasses both oneness and threeness is the one who created this universe. We need to take this doctrine from the shelves of orthodox academia and make it the basis for a true Christian definition of reality. Genesis 1 is a description of a harmonious universe made up of real diversity. Thus, what we need to ensure is harmony between the various aspects of reality rather than what the New Age movement offers, namely, the wishing away of diversity in favor of ultimate unity.

WHAT ARE THE MAIN TENETS OF HINDUISM?

Hinduism is a composite of complex and apparently contradictory beliefs. Many Hindu scholars accuse Christians (partly rightly) of reducing Hinduism's complexity to manageable proportions in order to critique it. I would suggest a model that would not only make a serious effort to accommodate the complex beliefs of Hinduism but also provide a framework for sharing Christ with those who have adopted its belief systems.

The model I suggest is a spectrum: at one end is polytheistic Hinduism, which involves the worship of many gods and goddesses; at the other end is pantheistic Hinduism, which promotes the idea of an infinite, unified impersonal reality and all else as totally illusory or as of secondary reality. The word *polytheism* comes from two Greek words—*polus* = "many" and *theos* = "God." *Pantheism* is arrived at by the adjective *pas* = "every" or "all" suffixed by the word *theos*. The idea is that all is God and God is all—there is no other reality. Physical reality, which to the Christian is created reality, is to the pantheist either totally illusory or is to be treated as a lower-level reality. The latter is at the heart of most of New Age beliefs and practices. The former—polytheism, which can be called popular Hinduism—has many similarities with Greek and Roman polytheisms, although the cultural context is very different. Pantheism on the other hand is based on speculative philosophy of the highest intellectual order and forms the backbone of the New Age movement.

Historically, polytheistic Hinduism antedates its pantheistic form. The ancient Hindu scriptures—called *Vedas,* embodiments of knowledge—at some points hint even of monotheism. The present-day worship of many gods and goddesses began as a veneration of the forces of nature, as did the polytheisms of Greece and Rome. This developed into a personification and deification of these forces with accompanying quasi-historical stories. It must be admitted that within the broad panorama of polytheism, one can discern threads of monotheism—nineteenth-century German philogist Friedrich Max Müller coined the term *henotheism* to signify worship of one God—whereby one of the deities is worshiped as possessing supreme power. This aspect of personal devotion to a personal deity should not be lost sight of in our categorizations of polytheistic Hinduism as idolatrous. The devotion shown by the Hindu in worship has few parallels in the often colorless cerebration we call worship of our all-worthy Creator. We would do well to learn from Paul who, while distressed at seeing the idols in Athens, could also discern the latent longing in the Athenians. (He employs this as a bridge in his outstanding lecture on the Areopagus; see Acts 17:22–23.) See also the treatment of the International Society of Krishna-Consciousness on pages 172–76.

It is also a well-attested fact that animal sacrifices formed an important part of ancient Hindu rituals as offerings meant to appease an offended deity. While the doctrine of sin and the atoning sacrifices are nowhere nearly as well developed as in the Old Testament, these parallels afford an important point of entry for the presentation of the gospel. It may be of interest to note that Brahmins who now are strict vegetarians were the priests who offered these sacrifices and ate of the oblation in token of its being accepted by deity. (It may not be out of place to note that all ancient religions were sacrifice-based—indicating an intuitive realization that humankind had somehow offended the powers that be, who therefore had to be appeased by the sacrifices.) The Christian should therefore be able to show the holiness of God and the inherent incapacity of human beings to meet the demands of this God and thus present the death of Jesus Christ as the only means to satisfy these demands, the only true culmination of the sacrifices of the ancients.

Tragically, the practice of this kind of polytheistic worship has led to class hierarchies that elevate the priests to the highest level. After the Brahminical caste are the warrior and merchant classes, and the last in the social ladder are the servant classes, some of whom are the untouchables. It has come to be believed that through the cycles of reincarnation (see "What Is Reincarnation?" page 171), the highest possible birth was into the human race, and within the human race the Brahmins were the highest. They would attain oneness with the Divine without much effort because of their service to deity during their tenure on earth.

A word may be in order concerning the demonic aspects of polytheism of any kind. Worship of personal deities may bring the worshiper into an occult encounter. Not uncommon are instances in which worshipers have been engaged by the Evil One and his minions in some form, particularly in terms of the benefits or harm that certain deities are known to bestow. In these instances, blood sacrifices to deities could form a crucial part of the worship. Satanism, which is on the ascendancy in all parts of the world today, has this common strand of the offering of blood as a token of life to engage the spiritual world.

The practice of idol worship is often accompanied by dedicating objects, places (such as temples, rivers, and mountaintops), and certain people (on some occasions) to various gods and goddesses. The activity of the demonic in such places and through such objects and persons is well attested. For example, Ramakrishna Paramahamsa, the teacher of Swami Vivekananda, is said to have invoked the spirit of *Kali,* the goddess of destruction, on his wife on a particular auspicious day. When she was thus possessed, he had sexual intercourse with her, claiming that he had thereby achieved union with the goddess. Whenever a creature is worshiped instead of the Creator (see Romans 1:25), moral corruption and spiritual perversity are not far behind. The recent preoccupation with and worship of Satan in the West could very well be the result of a godless pursuit of wealth and pleasure—and when these things don't satisfy the aspiration of the seeker, the only alternative is Satan, because God has already been ruled out.

Using the methodology outlined in the introduction to this chapter, the Christian should be able to identify with the inarticulated longings that lie within the heart of the Hindu. At one end of the spectrum is the desire to relate to personal deities who are unfortunately finite. At the other end, the need for an absolute is supplied by an entity that is unfortunately impersonal. The Christian answer to this spectrum of paradoxes is that God—Ultimate Reality—is infinite, personal, and relational. In fact, we need to redefine personality in *relational* terms rather than in uni-personal terms as is done in conventional theology. The faculties that constitute personality—intellect, emotion, and will—are theoretical, unactualized, and somewhat hollow in the absence of a functioning relationship. Thus, the triune nature of God can be a good place to start while sharing the gospel. The polytheistic Hindu will appreciate the centrality of relationality in the God of the Christian—one God in three persons (Father, Son, and Holy Spirit). The doctrine of sin can flow from an understanding of a ruptured relationship with God. Holiness itself is the supreme relationship of love within the Trinity (John 17:24; Romans 5:5). Even in Christian circles, holiness is often inadequately understood in ascetic terms of withdrawal—at which the Hindu is far more accomplished than the Christian can ever aspire to be!—rather than as involvement in robust relationships with God, fellow humans, and the rest of creation. We should be able to build on the ancient idea of sacrifices in polytheistic Hinduism to present the one full, perfect, and sufficient sacrifice of Jesus Christ as the fulfillment of all the attempted sacrifices of the past.

Hindus are often impressed by Christian involvement in social improvement, such as the work done by Mother Teresa. We need to see that Hinduism is a moralistic, salvation-by-works religion. It can be helpful to suggest (1) that humans can never live up to the moral requirements of their own consciences, not to mention the unutterably holy requirements of the triune God; (2) that good works done in expectation of rewards, say, a higher birth in a future reincarnation, cannot really be *good* works because there is an ulterior motive for performing them; but if God should save us free of cost, so to speak, in Christ and leave us on this planet to do good works, such works would be *really good* because we are in need of nothing more! This exposition of Ephesians 2:10 may appeal to the moralistic Hindu rather than the preaching of grace without any mention of works—at which the Hindu may go away, considering the gospel to be a cheap offer.

The pantheistic Hindu believes, as we've already seen, that Ultimate Reality is impersonal. This belief results in the clear conviction that personality is inferior to the ultimate impersonal reality. The Hindu's idea of salvation is, therefore, a desire to merge with the Infinite and, in a sense, lose his or her personality in the Infinite. We can point out to the Hindu that what makes us human is the capacity for free relationships, and losing our personalities is not going to be of much help! What we should strive for instead is the engagement of our personality in a lasting, fulfilling relationship—and this is precisely what God has offered in Jesus Christ.

It may also be important to note that the Christian emphasis on human sinfulness is sometimes mistaken by the Hindu to mean that Christianity offers a very poor image of our humanness. At this point, it may be necessary to admit that our own theology of the human race has often begun in Genesis 3 rather than in Genesis 1! We may need to redefine human sin in our own minds before we can present it correctly to the Hindu. The tragedy of human sin arises, not because the human being is constitutionally inferior to the rest of creation, but rather for the very opposite reason. Human rebellion against God is a cosmic tragedy only because humans are made in the image of God and placed by God in a position of dignity and honor (see Psalm 8:5–8) to rule over the rest of the earthly creation. The Hindu is likely to more easily identify with the reality of *human dignity* before being presented with the reality of sin; after all, this is the order of divine revelation in Genesis, isn't it? Sin, therefore, is a broken relationship with God—a relationship that alone afforded us identity, purpose, and dignity. While the detailing of practical sin may move nominal Christians in an evangelistic meeting, the philosophical Hindu is more likely to respond to the indignity of a broken relationship with Ultimate Reality—the infinite, personal, relational God.

WHAT IS TRANSCENDENTAL MEDITATION?

The term *Transcendental Meditation* (TM) was popularized by Maharishi Mahesh Yogi in the late 1960s. His diagnosis of the human predicament was that we who were actually part (or extension) of the infinite *Brahman* were unaware of the fact due to our ignorance *(avidya)* and preoccupation with mundane things. We needed to "transcend" the mundane by practice of the appropriate meditation—TM—in order to be able to find our union with the Infinite. (For more on this, see "What Does Yoga Mean and What Is the Teaching Behind It?" page 168.) This was classical pantheistic teaching of the earlier guru Sankara (A.D. 788–820).

Mahesh Yogi, however, suggested a very practical and down-to-earth way of meditation that didn't need any sophistication and practically no knowledge of Hinduism or speculative philosophy. In his *ashram* (prayer hall) in northern India, he would assign a monosyllabic word to each of the devotees in the language with which they were comfortable. Each devotee would have to repeat the assigned word audibly as a chant during all of one's waking moments. One could change over to a silent mode as long as the preoccupation was with that one word. After a few days, when the conscious mind was preoccupied with the word, the devotee was advised to expel the thought of that word so that the mind would become (theoretically) blank. In that moment of blankness, one could suddenly have an inward enlightenment *(Brahmavidya)* that one was an extension of Brahman. It was at this point that one would have transcended the transient in order to find the inward liberation that is the longing of the human heart.

A moment's reflection would show that the meditation recommended by the Maharishi involves an emptying of the mind—a *contentless* meditation. He argued that the clutter in our human minds came in the way of true knowledge of the Infinite. Another lesser-known philosopher, who lived most of his life in Oxford, England, and who died in 1986, was Dr. J. Krishnamurti. He located the human problem in our thoughts, a result of conditioning received during our lives as humans as we passed through various stages of intellectual development. He advocated "freedom from thoughts" as the means of liberation, although he did not perfect a technique as did the Maharishi. Practical as well as philosophical problems exist with this approach. Our minds are designed to think, and even to transcend (or get rid of) thinking we have to think! The guru who tells us that our thoughts are the problem has reached this conclusion and communicates it to us only by use of the very faculties that he decries. We are caught in a web of contradiction from which there is no escape. In fact, the logical conclusion of this philosophy is total silence—absence of communication. An ancient Indian scripture called the *Kenopanishad* has this unaffirmable quote: "He who speaks does not know, and he who knows does not speak"!

A demonic dimension may exist as well to this idea of contentless meditation. In a teaching recorded by Matthew, Jesus seems to be alluding to a situation in which the evil spirit has gone out of a person only to return and find "the house unoccupied, swept clean and put in order" (Matthew 12:43–45). This could be the state of a person whose mind is inactive in the passive sense after having been vacated of all other entities. In earlier times, we spoke of the idle mind as the "devil's workshop." Because transcendental and other forms of meditation are not anchored on objective truth, there is room not only for error but also for the occult. The devil delights to oppress (and even possess) the empty mind of the unbeliever where there is no seeking after the God of truth.

We will also do well to remember that meditation in this sense is "looking inward" to self rather than "looking outward" to God. Because the metaphysical teaching behind this meditation is that we are extensions of the Infinite Reality of Brahman, we are encouraged to look inward to realize this "truth" that we are part of the Infinite. The sin of the "morning star" was that he would "make [himself] like the Most High" (Isaiah 14:12–14). This attempt at self-realization as part of the

Infinite is the subtlest form of idolatry and thus an inevitable port of entry for the work of the devil.

In contrast, the triune God of the Christian faith is capable of eternal communication. He is a God who creates by speaking, so much so that the universe can be believed to be real and objective, just as a spoken word is. This God has created us capable of thinking and speaking. To belittle the faculty of thinking is to despise our created being. Christians in the West could react to the weird and exotic meditation techniques taught by New Agers by adopting an antimeditation stance. However, the answer to *wrong* meditation cannot be *no* meditation, but *right* meditation. We need to answer the *contentless* meditation of the New Age movement with *meditation on content*. The Bible enjoins us to meditate *on* God's Word (Psalm 1:2) and to think *on* things that are true, noble, right, pure, lovely, admirable, excellent, and praiseworthy (Philippians 4:8). Christians today are in danger of having the Word on our hard drives instead of in our hearts (Psalm 119:11).

We also need to move beyond an inductive cerebral understanding of God's Word to a subjective interaction with it in contemplation, whereby we become subjects in the narrative of God's revelation rather than objects who study it from the outside. The transforming work of the Holy Spirit becomes a reality in our lives only when the person of Jesus Christ confronts us in the Bible (2 Corinthians 3:18). A fuller understanding and application of 2 Corinthians 10:4–5 would involve an inner release of the power of God through the Scriptures so that even the mental strongholds of the thought-life are dismantled and brought into captivity to the obedience of Christ.

I trust that my reluctance to propound a whole new technique of meditating on the Bible is appreciated. I am loathe to absolutize a methodology and to trivialize the glorious theology of the Bible. I would suggest instead that the New Age emphasis on the subjective aspect of religious meditation should lead us to examine the legitimate subjectivity that the Bible encourages without straying to an unanchored mysticism. Then, and only then, shall we in theory and practice be able to answer the claims of the meditationists of the New Age.

Conclusion

The aspirations of classical Hinduism and modern-day New Age-ism point to two opposite poles in a theological spectrum. The first refers to finite personal gods, whereas the second emphasizes an infinite, impersonal reality. Thus, they are indicators that their followers long for *relationship* with and between gods on the one hand and for ultimate reality to be infinite on the other hand. These two requirements are more than adequately met in the God of the Bible, who is infinite and personal-relational because he is Trinity. As God's church, our final apologetic is the loving community of Christians that proclaims to the world that we are Christ's disciples (John 13:34–35).

QUESTIONS FOR REFLECTION AND DISCUSSION

1. What are the signposts you can look for in your acquaintances that may indicate they are looking for answers in a New Age religion?

2. Take some time to reflect on the magnitude of human sin as cosmic rebellion and the atoning sacrifice of Jesus Christ as sufficient in light of the inadequate ideas of sin and atonement in the religions discussed above. What thoughts come to mind?

3. Consider how the church (as well as the Christian family) can serve as an adequate model to reflect the unity and relationship of the Trinity and therefore be attractive to the followers of New Age religions. Discuss the implications with family members and fellow believers.

Chapter 9

Tough Questions about Yoga, Reincarnation, and Buddhism

L. T. Jeyachandran

As mentioned in chapter 8, Christians in the West face a culture that is increasingly influenced by New Age and other Eastern religious philosophies and practices. Additionally, we observed that Christians should not only look at the theological and philosophical answers proposed by these alternative religions, but also examine the existential context in which they have taken root.

For instance, Christianity unequivocally teaches that time is linear and that we human beings will be held responsible for the deeds done in this life since God will judge us at the end of this life (Hebrews 9:27). Belief in reincarnation or any other intermediate existence between the here and hereafter is thus ruled out in the tenets of the Christian faith. However, interest in reincarnation in a post–Christian Western context may arise for two reasons.

First, many people long to communicate with the dead. The desire of Bishop James Pike to speak to his dead son some years ago made headlines in the newspapers and precipitated a series of stories of those who allegedly successfully connected with those who had died. Second, reincarnation seems to be a preferable alternative to facing judgment at the hands of an infinitely holy God. Reincarnation offers an almost mechanistic cause and effect explanation for life after death without any particular moral accountability.

Some of these religions and practices also offer quick-fix relief to the stress-filled lifestyles of the twenty-first century. Yoga and meditation are thus said to be efficacious in alleviating the symptoms brought about by the fast pace of Western society. Let us then examine some of these teachings in detail.

WHAT DOES YOGA MEAN AND WHAT IS THE TEACHING BEHIND IT?

The simple *Sanskrit* term *yoga* actually means "union." As hinted at in chapter 8 (see "What Is Transcendental Meditation?" page 163), the human predicament is identified as ignorance of the fact that we are actually extensions of the infinite impersonal reality, *Brahman*. The adjective *impersonal* is applied to *Brahman* because ultimate reality is considered to be beyond qualities—beyond good and beyond evil—and is even said to be beyond being and beyond nonbeing. The reason for placing ultimate reality beyond the pale of qualifications is the (legitimate) concern that such qualifications would limit Brahman. The limitations implied are that words and qualities like *good* and *being* would exclude *nongood* and *nonbeing*. Brahman is therefore considered to be *nirguna*—without qualities. (I have stated that this concern to identify Brahman as beyond [or without] qualities is legitimate only because qualities appear to be interdependent and therefore relative. The answer to this rather weighty philosophical question is dealt with in the latter part of this answer.) The aim of the one who pursues truth should therefore be to realize union with this infinite reality in the midst of existential preoccupations, all of which seem to imprison the seeker within the walls of material and moral concerns.

The term *yoga* is used comprehensively and somewhat interchangeably to describe certain physical and mental techniques and exercises that facilitate the realization of the union of the finite with the infinite. Please note that union is not achieved—it need not be because it *is* a reality but is hidden from us because of a force of illusion called *maya*. What is needed, therefore, is a realization of the union that is already a reality rather than achieving a union that is not there to begin with.

To bring about this self-realization, a series of physical and meditational techniques are proposed. These are by no means uniform or similar and in fact can be quite diverse, depending on the particular school of yoga. The techniques are inaugurated in the form of physical exercises, although in some cases they may involve worship of the sun or the lotus form, the flower being the abode of the goddess of wealth, *Lakshmi*. These worship forms depend on the theological preferences of the Hindu school advocating the yoga. In order not to offend Western sensibilities, yoga these days is purveyed without any theological overtones but only as a series of physical exercises, and in most cases, these exercises can have salutary physical effects.

Yoga teachers often encourage their students to meditate—without necessarily telling them what to meditate on or how to do it. They may even tell Christian students to meditate on Jesus Christ! The idea, of course, is that one thinks about and reflects on the subject of meditation. This in itself is of no great concern. However, as one advances in the yoga course, one is often called on to be increasingly involved in a meditation that entails vacating the mind. In the July 16, 2001, issue of *Time* (Asia) magazine, Hindu guru Bharat Thakur scoffed at the Western practice of yoga with purely physical health as the goal. He divides the practice into two parts—the external and the internal. The external involves the physical, and his point of view is that the West is interested only in this aspect without wanting to enter into the internal. His argument is that yoga is a complete package and that one has no option to separate the two. To enter into the internal, he suggests the following:

> You need a true master to take you into spiritual yoga. Someone who has walked inside himself. Such a master will ask: Now friend, you have known the body, you have known your breath, your mind,

so what next? After that begins the trip to the unknown where the master makes the student gradually aware at every stage, where you know that you are not the body or the mind and not even the soul. That is when you get the first taste of *moksha* [i.e., salvation], or enlightenment. It is the sense of the opening of the silence, the sense where you lose yourself and are happy doing it, where for the first time your ego has merged with the superconsciousness. You feel you no longer exist, for you have walked into the valley of death. And if you start walking more and more in this valley, you become freer.

It is a trip from you to no you. A trip from the known to unknown. From the valley of total knowledge, stuff and ego to utter surrender where nothing remains in you but pure consciousness. You go to a stage where you are totally free of fear or dying. Or living. And that's what a yogi means in India. It is someone who has moved from body to the mind, to the soul, to awareness, to the subtle surrender to the superconsciousness. Next time you head for a yoga class, ask yourself whether you are ready to be a seeker of the path.[1]

This quote from a New Age guru illustrates several points:

- The physical is meaningless and is to be transcended for true mastery. This should not be confused by the Christian with Paul's statement in 1 Corinthians 9:27. Paul is referring to control over a very real physical body. He does not say that the physical is intrinsically evil or unreal and has to be bypassed in order to attain *moksha*.

- The logical and rational are to give way to the nonrational or, better still, the suprarational. As long as we use our minds, we will remain in a lower state. The epistemology of pantheism (which is the ground of yoga) is thus unknowable and nonaffirmable.

- When used by yogis, words like *surrender* are meaningless, because there is no entity or personality to surrender to. The word is often used to denote the utter nothingness that seems to be what ultimate reality is all about.

- Similarly, *enlightenment* would not mean objectively knowing something or someone. Instead, it is used to refer to self-realization, to one's oneness with the Absolute Brahman.

The Christian answer to this particularly strong onslaught on the truth should be rooted in the ontology (being), morality, and epistemology (knowing) of the Trinity. It is only in the triune God that we have meaningful being-in-relationship. The Western (sometimes Christian) emphasis on individualism plays straight into the jaws of this philosophy. We even need to redefine personality, not on the basis of stand-alone abstracts such as reason, emotion, and will, but rather on actualization of these qualities in relationship with God, other humans, and the impersonal creation. Similarly, morality for the Christian epitomized by love is the character of the relationship within the Trinity (read John 17:24 with Romans 5:5—the Father loves the Son through the Holy Spirit). Again, individualized morality, described in phrases such as "personal holiness," cannot stand the relativized ethics that this philosophy supplies. Holiness has to be understood to be interpersonal in God as well as in us who are made in his image. Also, knowledge is rooted in the eternal mutual knowledge within the Trinity (Matthew 11:27) rather than in the self-realization bandied about by New Agers. The Christian emphasis on objective knowledge must include the personal relational knowledge with God and his creation.

Therefore, the Christian answer to yoga is a knowable relationship with God evidenced by a loving relationship with others and the world. This is eternal life (John 17:3), and the Law and the Prophets are fulfilled in the keeping of these commandments (Matthew 22:34–40).

WHAT IS REINCARNATION?

Reincarnation is the belief that a being (human, animal, vegetable, or mineral), after cessation of existence on earth, will experience a new birth and enter existence again in the form of another being. This belief is based on two assumptions: First, time is cyclical—sometimes phrased as "time-lessness"—and whatever happens will happen again. Second, the class of birth depends on the deeds done by the being in the previous birth.

Belief in reincarnation is common to Hinduism and Buddhism, although the mechanics are different. Both polytheistic and pantheistic forms of Hinduism approach reincarnation in somewhat different ways. The Hindu believes that the individual soul, the *jivatman,* is an extension of the eternal soul, the *paramatman,* or simply *atman.* One's identity in any particular life is the *jivatman* in a form earned by deeds *(karma)* in the previous birth. When a *jivatman* transmigrates at cessation of existence of that particular form, it may begin existence in a totally new form, again decided by karma—and so the cycle goes on.

In polytheistic Hinduism, gods and goddesses themselves are treated as incarnations (or reincarnations), and thus their human history need not necessarily be absolute. This also shows why a polytheist Hindu is not too disturbed by the absence of exemplary moral qualities in the pantheon. There is in recent times, however, a development in which one of the gods, *Krishna,* who in classical Hinduism is an incarnation—in fact, one of nine with some devotees looking forward to a perfect tenth incarnation—of the god of preservation, *Vishnu,* has been elevated to the Infinite-Personal level. This is the same theological status given to God in Islam, Judaism, and Christianity. The devotees of this understanding of *Krishna* belong to the International Society of Krishna-Consciousness (ISKCON). I will say more about this group below (see pages 175–76).

The polytheistic idea of salvation is to reach the highest of possible births, considered by many to be *birth as a Brahmin.* Thereafter, because of performing religious rites and duties, visiting holy places, bathing in sacred rivers, and offering oblations and worship *(pujas)* at various shrines, the devotee attains *moksha* (salvation). Good works are often understood, not as moral behavior to be measured against the just requirements of a holy deity, but as the performance of religious duties carried out meticulously in accordance with the rules laid down in the *Vedas* (ancient Hindu scriptures). Socially, the practice of Brahminism as a way of life has fallen into some disrepute because of the caste discrimination by Brahmins against those of "lower" births. Thus, pilgrimage to holy places is undertaken by all levels of Hindu society, although there are areas in temples and rivers where the lowest castes are not permitted to enter even now. Performance of religious duties in temples is still largely the duty of Brahmin priests.

The concept of salvation among polytheists is somewhat vague. While it definitely includes an escape from the cycle of rebirths, it does not spell out clearly whether it is an identity-less merger with the Infinite or communion with the Personal. ISKCON devotees would clearly side with the latter and speak of salvation as communion with *Krishna,* whereas the New Age branch of pantheists and some popular (polytheistic) Hindus would take the position of the former—absorption into the infinite Brahman.

Pantheistic Hinduism treats personality as an inferior manifestation of the Impersonal (already stated above). Thus, belief in personal deities is considered a primitive form of understanding the Absolute Brahman because these deities themselves are lower manifestations of Ultimate Reality. However, pantheists encourage polytheists to be devoted to these gods and goddesses until they reach enlightenment, when they will break out of the cycle of rebirths—called *Karma Samsara.* According to pantheists, therefore, bondage to the karmic cycles of reincarnation is an indication that *brahmavidya* has not been attained. In other words, my self-consciousness as a human being is proof that I am still part of this cycle and that I need to be liberated by means of true union (yoga) with the Infinite Brahman.

The idea of reincarnation is now being challenged by some contemporary Hindu scholars on the following grounds: First, there is the problem of evaluating good karma (works). If a being could belong to all categories of life and nonlife, how could one attribute good karmic behavior to impersonal creatures?

Second, there are two problems for the pantheist—one is that all reality is one and therefore karma of one creature cannot be distinguishable from that of another. Also, the pantheist insists on the absolute Impersonal and therefore cannot find any ground for the standard for measuring karmic (moral) behavior.

Third, and half seriously, some have commented that, due to the deteriorating moral lifestyle of our present generation, very few humans would be born "again" into a human birth. Animals and granite slabs have no basis to live a moral life anyway, and they cannot therefore aspire to become humans. How is it, then, that we have this huge population explosion?

The pantheist normally takes recourse to a cause and effect approach while discussing karma. He or she would say that, because every action has a reaction, the karma of our future life is the reaction to what we did in the previous birth, and we are not to give moral overtones to this phenomenon. I have heard some pantheists even refer to Galatians 6:7—"A man reaps what he sows." They would, of course, choose to ignore the moral context in which Paul makes this statement.

The Christian can capitalize on the teaching of karma. Sometimes in preaching the gospel of grace we have not adequately dealt with good works. At the great white throne judgment portrayed in Revelation 20:11–15, human beings are judged on the basis of what they have *done*. While it is correct to say that hell is the destination of those who have rejected Christ, we should not gloss over the fact that the "books" in this passage are the records of the deeds of humans by which they are judged. Christian salvation is therefore the intervention of the incarnate God, Jesus Christ, to break the karmic cycle by bearing our karmic debt, as it were, because by our karma we never would have been able to please an unutterably holy God. His own character is the standard, then, that judges humans. Those who escape the judgment do so not by the lowering of the standard, not by attaining it (because this is impossible), but by the vicarious meeting of the requirement by Jesus Christ.

We also can use the findings of science to counter the idea of the cyclical nature of history. Of the dimensions we are familiar with—the three spatial dimensions of length, breadth, and height plus the one extra dimension of time—only time is unidirectional. In other dimensions, we can travel in two opposite directions—right or left, forward or backward, up or down—but in time we move only toward the future. This strongly suggests that time is linear rather than circular. This property of time has fascinated and puzzled physicists, who have coined the phrase "arrow of time" to describe it. Therefore what Hebrews 9:27 says—"man is destined to die once, and after that to face judgment"—is more in accord with the scientific understanding of time than proposing that there is an endless series of births and rebirths.

A word needs to be said about the International Society of Krishna-Consciousness. While I would not say that belief in Krishna as Infinite-Personal God is the logical next step in the evolution of Hinduism because of the conflicts and contradictions encountered above, it would be fair to conclude that the human heart longs for personal relationship and fulfillment—and these things are not addressed by the idea of reincarnation. The *bhakti* movement in Hinduism, which has been around for centuries, is the outworking of devotion to God and has found its recent manifestation in ISKCON. Followers of this group can be identified by their shaven heads—sometimes a tuft of hair is sported. They are not ashamed to walk down the streets chanting, *"Hare Rama, Hare Krishna,"* worship terms ascribing honor to the gods *Rama* and *Krishna*. This group does not believe in reincarnation or in absorption into the impersonal Brahman. They teach that by being devoted to Krishna in the present life, humans will be able to enjoy eternal communion with him in the hereafter.

My 1997 encounter with some ISKCON devotees may be relevant as to how bridges can be built to share the gospel with people who hold views that are so different from the gospel's teaching. This small group of Ph.D. scholars in one of the premier engineering institutions in India had asked me to speak on the subject "God and Science." But somehow the dialogue turned to a comparison between Jesus Christ and Krishna. For every single aspect of Christ I shared with them, they could find a comparable one in Krishna. They eventually asked me to say something about the Christian view of heaven, because they claimed that some of the ancient Hindu writings did speak of Krishna seated in all his perfection in heavenly splendor. I agreed with them that Revelation 21 contained a spectacular description of heaven, but there seemed to be a fundamental divergence: over against the "perfect" Krishna, my Christ was "imperfect"; he still had the wounds he had received on the cross. For the first time during the dialogue, there was shocked silence as I proceeded to share the gospel—that outside of the crucified Christ, there was no hope of eternal communion with God for human beings because of their sinful state. The ISKCON movement, in promising heavenly bliss without going through the interminable cycles of births and rebirths, did not reckon with the unfitness of sinful humanity to dwell in the company of the moral beauty of God displayed in the splendor of heaven.

Today's ideas of astral travel and transmigration of souls is more in line with our appetite for power and knowledge to control other people and events; these ideas have fit in well with some of the longstanding theological assumptions of Hinduism. It is fair to issue a warning at this point that some of the reported instances of little children recounting the exact details of their past life are more likely the result of demonization than proof of the theory of reincarnation. The lust for power and the accompanying interest in the occult evidenced these days can lead to direct encounters with the powers of darkness, more than we'd care to think.

WHAT ARE THE BELIEFS OF BUDDHISM?

The Buddha ("the enlightened one") was born as Siddhartha Gautama in Lumbini (in present-day Nepal) in a princely family of the Sakya clan. The date of his birth is variously placed between 624 B.C and 448 B.C. The commonly accepted date is 560 B.C. He lived a protected life, as his father did not want his sensitive son to be exposed to the harsh realities of human existence. Legend has it that during surreptitious visits to the outside world, he came across, on consecutive days, a sick man, an old man, and a dead man being carried to the crematorium.

Having concluded that life was nothing but suffering resulting in sickness, aging, and death, Siddhartha renounced his life as a householder (with a young wife and a baby boy) at the age of twenty-nine and began to wander through the plains of eastern India in search of the truth. He is said to have received enlightenment at the age of thirty-six on the night of a full moon in the month of May. This happened in Gaya in what is now the Bihar State of India. During a similar full-moon night in the following July, he delivered his first discourse near the Hindu holy city of Varanasi, introducing the world to the four noble truths. His death at the age of eighty is referred to by his followers as *Parinibbana* (Pali; Sanskrit, *Parinirvana*), or final release.

One hundred years after Buddha's death, the second council of Buddhist monks met at Vaishali, where the first schism occurred in ancient Buddhism. Those who did not accept the writing of the early Buddhists as authoritative branched off to form the *Mahayana* ("Greater Vehicle") school of Buddhism, which became the dominant religion in China, Tibet, Japan, and Korea. Those who subscribed to the Buddhist scriptures constituted the *Theravada* school ("School of Elders," also called, somewhat derogatorily, *Hinayana* = "Lesser Vehicle"). This school has flourished in Sri Lanka, Myanmar, and Thailand. Buddhism can be said to have arisen out of a reaction to the Hinduism of those days possibly because of its caste system. Early Buddhists were persecuted and driven out of India—the reason why Buddhism as a religion did not flourish in India but has done well in other Asian countries.

The Buddha's four noble truths are as follows:

1. the noble truth of *dukkha* (suffering, dissatisfaction, stress): life is fundamentally fraught with disappointment of every description.
2. the noble truth of the cause of *dukkha:* the cause of this dissatisfaction is *tanha*—craving in all its forms.
3. the noble truth of the cessation of *dukkha:* an end to all dissatisfaction can be found through relinquishment and abandonment of craving.
4. the noble truth of the path leading to the cessation of *dukkha:* there is a method of achieving the end of all dissatisfaction, namely, the Noble Eightfold Path.

To each of these noble truths, the Buddha assigned a specific task for the practitioner: the first noble truth is to be comprehended; the second is to be abandoned; the third is to be realized; the fourth is to be developed. The full realization of the third noble truth paves the way for the penetration of *Nibbana* (Pali; Sanskrit, *Nirvana*), the transcendent freedom by total annihilation (and abnegation [literally, nakedness]) of the self that stands as the final goal of all of the Buddha's teachings.

The last of the noble truths, the Noble Eightfold Path, contains a prescription for the relief of our unhappiness and for our eventual release, once for all, from the painful and wearisome cycle of birth and death *(samsara)* to which—through our own ignorance (Pali, *avijja;* Sanskrit, *avidya*) of the four noble truths—we have been bound for countless eons. The Noble Eightfold Path offers a comprehensive practical guide to the development of these wholesome qualities and skills in the human heart that must be cultivated in order to bring the practitioner to the final goal, namely, the supreme freedom and happiness of *Nibbana.* The eight qualities to be developed are right view, right resolve, right speech, right action, right livelihood, right effort, right mindfulness, and right concentration.

In practice, the Buddha taught the Noble Eightfold Path to his followers according to a system of gradual training, beginning with the development of *sila,* or virtue (right speech, right action, and right livelihood, which are summarized in practical form by suitable precepts), followed by the development of *samadhi,* or concentration and mental cultivation (right effort, right mindfulness, and right concentration), culminating in the development of *panna,* or wisdom (right view and right resolve). The practice of *dana,* or generosity, serves as a support at every step along the path, as it helps foster the development of a compassionate heart and counters the heart's habitual tendency to craving.

Progress along the path does not follow a simple linear trajectory. Rather, development of each aspect of the Noble Eightfold Path encourages the refinement and strengthening of the others, leading the practitioner ever forward in an upward spiral of spiritual maturity that culminates in awakening.

Seen from another point of view, the long journey on the path to awakening begins in earnest with the first tentative stirrings of right view, the first flickerings of wisdom by which one recognizes both the validity of the first noble truth and the inevitability of the law of *kamma* (Pali; Sanskrit, *karma*), the universal law of cause and effect. Once one begins to see that harmful actions inevitably bring about harmful results and wholesome actions bring about wholesome results, the desire to live a skillful, morally upright life and to take seriously the practice of *sila* grows naturally. The confidence built from this preliminary understanding inclines the follower to put his or her trust more deeply in the teachings. The follower becomes a Buddhist upon expressing an inner resolve to "take refuge" in the Triple Gem:

1. the *Buddha*—both the historical Buddha and one's own innate potential for awakening
2. the *Dhamma* (Pali; Sanskrit, *Dharma* = "teaching")—both the teachings of the historical Buddha and the ultimate Truth toward which they point
3. the *Sangha*—both the monastic community that has protected the teachings and put them into practice since the Buddha's day, as well as all those who have achieved at least some degree of awakening

With one's feet thus firmly planted on the ground by taking refuge in the "Triple Gem," and with an admirable friend (Pali, *kalyanamitta;* Sanskrit, *kalyanamitra* = "friend interested in one's welfare") to help show the way, one can set out along the path, confident that one is indeed following in the footsteps left by the Buddha himself.

Buddhism, as originally taught by the Buddha and the school of elders, does not refer at all to a personal deity or deities and can be regarded as atheistic (denying the existence of deity). The *Theravada* form is similar to pantheistic Hinduism in a number of ways. Both are reticent to admit a personal deity and seem to be dealing with impersonal forces. The key word is *wisdom,* not in the sense of laying hold of something objective, but in the context of self-realization. The modern school of Zen Buddhism, though not historically linked to the *Theravada* branch, majors in the subject of meditation, which incidentally is also recommended by the *Theravada* school. The word *Zen* is actually a corrupt form of the Sanskrit *Dhyan,* meaning "meditation." A corresponding Chinese word, *Shan,* conveys the same meaning. In Zen, as in TM, the idea of meditation is that of the contentless, vacuous variety that could lead to "wisdom." The individual is in a world of his or her own, and emancipation is by self-effort only.

The *Mahayana* form on the other hand has certain features in common with polytheistic popular Hinduism. Both consider the need for saviors—in *Mahayana,* the Buddha himself is considered a savior and salvation is by grace. Petitionary prayers are common in both. In some Buddhist temples, there are places to offer incense to Hindu deities. Although these

Hindu deities are not allowed into the Buddhist *sanctum sanctorum* (holy of holies, or inner shrine), prayers made to them are considered efficacious.

Some of the apologetic methods suggested in chapter 8 (see "What Are the Main Tenets of Hinduism?" page 158) would apply mutatis mutandis to *Mahayana* and *Theravada* forms of Buddhism. In addition, we can point out that any analysis of life on purely negative criteria will invariably run into trouble. For example, to say that everything is suffering, one should have some idea of joy and pleasure. We see suffering as suffering only in contrast to something that can be enjoyed. We would not know suffering as suffering if everything were indeed suffering! It is similar to C. S. Lewis's musings before his conversion:

> My argument against God was that the universe seemed so cruel and unjust. But how had I got this idea of *just* and *unjust?* A man does not call a line crooked unless he has some idea of a straight line. What was I comparing this universe with when I called it unjust? If the whole show was bad from A to Z, so to speak, why did I, who was supposed to be part of the show, find myself in such violent reaction against it? A man feels wet when he falls into water, because man is not a water animal; a fish would not feel wet. Of course I could have given up my idea of justice by saying it was nothing but a private idea of my own. But if I did that, my argument against God collapsed too—for the argument depended on saying that the world was really unjust, not simply that it did not happen to please my fancies. Thus in the very act of trying to prove that God did not exist—in other words, that the whole of reality was senseless—I found I was forced to assume that one part of reality—namely my idea of justice—was full of sense. Consequently atheism turns out to be too simple. If the whole universe has no meaning, we should never have found out that it has no meaning; just as, if there were no light in the universe and therefore no creatures with eyes, we should never have known that it was dark. *Dark* would be a word without meaning.[2]

As we contemplate this quote, we ought not to mistake Buddhism to have logically concluded that God does not exist because of the first noble truth—that everything is suffering. God simply does not figure in the writings of the Buddha. We can, on the other hand, point out from a philo-sophical point of view that pain is understandable only against the back-drop of pleasure—and both are realities in our existence. We should therefore encourage the Buddhist to look for the causes of suffering else-where. What's more, we should be able to show that, even at the pragmatic level, there is much in life that is good, and there are good people who try to alleviate suffering. Even the Buddhist teaching to practice *dana* (gen-erosity) is a tacit admission that suffering can and is being alleviated in this world of suffering.

There is an admirable fact in the second noble truth—the location of the reason for suffering in *tanha* (craving). The apostle John warns of "the cravings of sinful man, the lust of his eyes and the boasting of what he has and does" (1 John 2:16). However, the third noble truth runs into a con-tradiction. Relinquishment of craving can itself be a craving; that is, the desire to get rid of craving is itself a desire! An existence without desire is an existential as well as a logical contradiction. Instead, we need to focus our desires on an object worthy of our desire (see Psalm 27:4). Similarly, the fourth noble truth lays down the basis for an admirable lifestyle but offers little to actually execute it. We come back to the serious weakness of *know-ing* what is right and being unable to *do* it.

We need to help our Buddhist friends become capable of identifying with the real problem of suffering and indicate to them the connection between suffering and the existence of moral evil as a state of rebellion against a morally holy God. We can address the problem of suffering by pointing to a God who identifies with us in suffering—the devastating suf-fering experienced on the cross. True enlightenment for us will be a face-to-face encounter with a loving Savior, Jesus Christ, when our journey on earth is ended.

A final word about Buddhist reincarnation is in order. While the Hindu maintains the identity of the individual soul in the process of transmigra-tion, the Buddhist believes that the soul at death dissipates into five essences and then reassembles in the new cycle of life. However, there is no guar-antee for the *identity of the person,* as there may be in the case of the Hindu.

Thus, this particular belief of Buddhism can lead the adherent to a deep sense of insecurity regarding his or her identity. The Christian has a specific answer to this issue: We are not only known by our Creator from our mothers' wombs; he has made sure that there is a room—a place—where only we will fit and no other. Thus, our identity is preserved in our relationship with God through the Lord Jesus Christ.

Conclusion

A number of Hindus and Buddhists have given their lives to Christ, not through philosophical arguments, but through the genuine love and friendship offered by their Christian friends. Over against the emphasis of yoga as merger with some indefinable reality, we can offer true relationship with the Infinite God through Jesus Christ and exemplify it through our own enjoyment of that sacred bond. Buddhists belabor the point that their religion is *not* life-denying religion offering nothing more than total nihilism—but it is hard to escape the conclusion that this is what the Buddha taught.

Sadly, we sometimes portray Christianity as mere asceticism with a Christian slant and thus reduce to personal devotion alone what it means to follow Christ. The strongest argument against the attraction of Eastern religions lies not merely in an individual pursuit of Christian holiness but rather in the practice of a visible and demonstrable *Christian community*.

QUESTIONS FOR REFLECTION AND DISCUSSION

1. Is there anything wrong with yoga that focuses on its physically therapeutic benefits?

2. What is the simplest way to demonstrate practically that this life is really important and that we ought not to expect a second chance to do better?

3. In a world of materialistic pursuits, how can the Christian adopt and live out the life-affirmative emphasis of the Christian faith without becoming prosperity oriented?

Chapter 10

Tough Questions about Black Islam

Robert White

I remember attending a Nation of Islam meeting when I was a freshman student at Tuskegee University in the late 1980s. Prior to enrolling in college, I had a unique religious experience and felt comfortable with my Christian beliefs, but I was curious to learn about other belief systems. I was not prepared, however, for what I was about to endure. Before the Nation of Islam meeting began, I was ushered into an adjacent room by some guys I recognized from the dorm. Once in the room, I was searched "for my protection" and ushered into the room where the meeting was held. I soon noticed that the ushers were separating the audience based on gender. A few minutes later, a man about my age entered the room with five other guys, and the meeting was called to order. After a prayer, an offering, and a recitation from the Qur'an, the minister began to speak. He spoke with pride and confidence. At first his message was no different from the one I heard on Sunday morning in church. But the Muslim minister especially caught my attention when he mentioned the position of black men in America and ways in which black people could change the conditions of their community.

As the speech progressed, I noticed that the minister slowly and subtly shifted his attention to a more controversial theme. He began to attack the Bible and urged us to stop worshiping the "white Jesus." He also claimed that the white man was not human but was a devil and an enemy of God. He finally introduced a man named Master Fard Muhammad as being the final prophet of God and the Comforter spoken of in Scripture. The minister's final request was that we reflect on what we heard and examine the reasons for our beliefs up to this point. He concluded by inviting us to a follow-up meeting the next week, since there was clearly no reason to deny Islam. While his speech was provocative, I was left with a question: Is Christianity truly a white man's religion, or am I being deceived?

After that meeting, I was confused, and I temporarily denied everything white, including the picture of the "white Jesus" on my grandmother's wall. Although I had white friends at the time, I began to withdraw from them and initiated the process of reassessment. I rethought my entire life, my fears, my anxieties, and the God I had chosen to serve. Going to this meeting made me research the Scriptures and seek answers to the issues the speaker raised. But after having done my own "soul searching," I chose to stick with Christ, because his promises best represent my expectations for life. I discovered that I did not believe in Christ because my parents did. Rather, I learned that God, through Christ, had a plan for me and that he was the person motivating me to search the Scriptures. But how many other young Christians come to this conclusion? That same year I saw several of my friends convert to Islam and follow the teachings of Elijah Muhammad. Indeed, Paul in his letter to the Galatians gives a warning not to receive any other gospel that is preached (even if it is given by a well-dressed, articulate fellow or by an angel in a cave!):

> But even if we, or an angel from heaven, should preach to you a gospel contrary to what we have preached to you, he is to be cursed! As we have said before, so I say again now, if any man is preaching to you a gospel contrary to what you received, he is to be accursed!
>
> *Galatians 1:8–9 NASB*

WHAT IS THE CURRENT CLIMATE OF THE CHURCH?

Martin Luther King Jr. once said, "Yes, I see the church as the body of Christ. But, oh! How we have blemished and scarred that body through social neglect and through fear of being nonconformists."[1] Christian clergy like King have always played a major role in the African-American community, particularly in the struggle for civil rights. Historically, the African-American church has had the dual distinction of being the center for the Christian faith and an institution of social change. In turn, the African-American pastor has been the voice of reason for the black community and a spokesperson for human rights. Still, even though the church has been at the forefront of social change, the black church has seen its share of black Christians fall prey to the influences of non-Christian organizations.

Because the church's role in the current civil agenda for African Americans has decreased significantly, some activists have begun to meet in other venues that are considered less threatening and more conducive to diversity. In such meetings, black Christians are warned "to leave their religion at the door," and praying in the name of Jesus has been replaced with nonsectarian prayers. Is this a problem? Yes, because this restriction gives other religious groups, like the Baha'i and certain Islamic fringe groups, the luxury of propagating their religious ideas under the auspices of a less threatening heading called *social consciousness*. The popularity of black Islamic groups, especially among young people, gives rise to the need for black preachers and church leaders to develop a Christian response to the enticing non-Christian messages being communicated in the community. (For further discussion, see "How Might the Church Reach Out to Black Muslims," page 199).

To understand the social dynamic of black religion (Islam), an understanding of the role Christianity played in the struggle of black people is important. The greatest tragedy of early American Christendom was the failure of white preachers to denounce slavery and the practice of segregation. Rev. Fred Price, pastor of the Crenshaw Christian Center in Los Angeles, made this observation in a recent interview:

The problem with the church is not the Bible. It's those who have interpreted it, or, more accurately, misinterpreted it. Some people are saying that because people took the Bible, manipulated its message, and used it as a reason to justify the enslavement of and the mistreating of a race of people for no other reason than the color of their skin, we ought to dump the Bible. But the Bible has not been the problem; it's been the so-called purveyors of biblical teaching.[2]

Although many slaves and subsequent generations accepted Christianity, the slaves viewed the kind of Christianity espoused by the white missionaries to be a tool of oppression. Many believed that accepting Jesus Christ was synonymous with accepting the Western social order or some type of geopolitical agenda—a point of contention that still exists today. The only burden white church leaders have in rectifying this situation is to make sure they don't repeat the past by surrendering to the domestic pressures of racial difference and racial prejudice.

WHAT MAKES RELIGION "BLACK"?

America has placed a high level of importance on racial distinction. As recently as the 1960s, American life was separated into two domains—black and white. There were black and white water fountains, black and white schools, black and white movie houses, black and white jobs, and black and white religion. In particular, *black* religion can be defined as the spiritual patterns and practices of black people in America that have developed over the course of four hundred years. Black religion is also a continuity of the spiritual practices of African people. So Black Islam can be defined as *the social philosophy of Islam articulated through the African-American experience.*

Because the status of Negro people in America has improved over time, there is a need for periodic self-identification. While European immigrants, for example, tend to express a dual identity that encompasses United States citizenship as well as their point of origin, black people have embraced their U.S. citizenship reluctantly and have often accepted the identity placed on them by the American social order. The terms

Negro, colored, and *black* are not synonyms but do signify key features of African existence at various points in the evolving American social order. Without the experiences that black people have suffered in America, which made racial distinction a cornerstone of existence, there would be no need to designate religions in terms of black or white. It should also be noted that most black churches were founded after Negroes were refused access to white churches.

Theology tends to express thoughts about God in human terms, and *black* theology in particular is always related to historical events and the cultural experiences of black people. Note the words of James Cone, author of the book *God of the Oppressed:*

> White theologians built logical systems; black folks told tales. Whites debated the validity of infant baptism or the issue of predestination and free will—blacks recited biblical stories about God leading the Israelites from Egyptian bondage, Joshua and the battle of Jericho, and the Hebrew children in the fiery furnace. White theologians argued about the general status of religious assertions in view of the development of science generally and Darwin's *Origin of Species* in particular; blacks were more concerned about their status in American society and its relation to the biblical claim that Jesus came to set the captives free. Whites thought the Christian view of salvation was largely "spiritual" and sometimes rational, but usually separated from the concrete struggle of freedom in this world. Black thought was largely eschatological and never abstract, but usually related to blacks' struggle against earthly oppression.[3]

Enough evidence exists to prove that a significant portion of slaves who arrived on the shores of America were Muslim. For example, missionaries from South Carolina, Georgia, and Louisiana spoke of slaves praying to Allah and abstaining from eating pork. But the slaves soon adopted the religion of their masters and tailored its basic tenets to reflect their experience. Now, after four hundred years of Christianity, many African Americans are reverting back to the religions their forefathers espoused before coming to the shores of America.

WHO FOUNDED THE BLACK ISLAMIC MOVEMENT?

The Nation of Islam has been the most popular and controversial black Islamic movement among African Americans. But the Nation of Islam is actually the perpetuation of two previous black Islamic movements. While people from outside the United States started organizations like the Ahmadiyya, other movements started by black Americans gave the Islamic genre a more Afrocentric aura.[4] In Newark, New Jersey, in 1913, Timothy Drew established the Moorish Science Temple Divine and National Movement (changed to Moorish Science Temple of America in 1925). Claiming to be a disciple of Allah, he taught an aesthetic approach to unlocking the keys to the significance of racial difference. Later calling himself Noble Drew Ali, he said that the terms *Negro* and *black* signified death and that a more appropriate name for African people would be Moorish or Asiatic.[5] Ali believed that salvation would be found in a proper interpretation of the self and the denial of false identities. The primary focus of the Moorish Science Temple was the discovery of the authentic self, and the organization did not practice racial separation per se.

After Drew Ali would come Wali (or Wallace) D. Fard, who some say was a Caucasian man from Arabia. Fard's successor Elijah Muhammad made this observation:

> The Mahdi (Fard Muhammad) is a world traveler. He told me that he had traveled the world over and that he had visited North America for 20 years before making himself known to us, his people, whom he came for. He could speak 16 languages and could write 10 of them. He visited every inhabited place on the earth and had pictured and extracted the languages of the people on Mars and had knowledge of all life in the universe. He could recite by heart the histories of the world as far back as 150,000 years and knew the beginning and end of all things.[6]

While peddling door-to-door like the Muslim missionaries did in Africa during the thirteenth century, Fard spread his message of Islam. In 1930 he changed his name to Wali D. Fard Muhammad and established the

Temple of Islam in Detroit, Michigan. After recruiting more than eight thousand members, Fard departed as mysteriously as he had emerged. Following his disappearance, his organization split into two groups—the Temple of Islam, headed by Abdul Muhammad, and the Nation of Islam, headed by Elijah Muhammad. Although Abdul Muhammad disagreed about Fard Muhammad's being the messiah, to the followers of Elijah Muhammad, the disappearance of Wali D. Fard Muhammad was a fulfillment of a *hadith* (an authoritative saying of the prophet Muhammad) and biblical prophecy.[7] For a more comprehensive analysis of the early black Islamic movement and black theology, a study of the works of Cain Hope Felder, James Cone, Carl Ellis, and C. E. Lincoln is helpful.[8]

WHO WAS RESPONSIBLE FOR BRINGING THE MESSAGE OF BLACK ISLAM TO THE FOREFRONT?

After Fard Muhammad's departure, Elijah Muhammad began to preach that European Christianity was highly influenced by European imperialism and American capitalism and was not in the best interest of any Negro people. In his book *The Supreme Wisdom,* Elijah Muhammad wrote, "The so-called Negroes must get away from the old slavery teaching that Jesus, who died two thousand years ago, is still alive somewhere waiting and listening to their prayers."

But the most controversial of Elijah Muhammad's teachings had to do with the origin of the white race. Following the theories of Fard Muhammad, whom some claim was Caucasian, Elijah Muhammad taught that the white man was a devil and was the offspring of a mad scientist named Yacub. This teaching was controversial in America and incited rebuke from the universal Islamic community as well. According to Elijah Muhammad, Yacub was an enemy of Allah who was expelled from Mecca. Yacub genetically engineered a legion of "white devils" who would later wage war against Allah. But Allah prevailed, and the final place of exile for the white devils was the region now known as Europe. Elijah Muhammad further claimed that America was corrupting Negro people and forbidding intermarriage with whites. He declared that total separation from white culture was the only alternative for African Americans. Elijah Muhammad's message was shunned by most black intellectuals but was well received by members of the black political and entertainment community. According to a report in the February 20, 1960, *Los Angeles Herald Dispatch,* close to 150 African Americans denounced Christianity and embraced Islam at a Nation of Islam rally in Los Angeles.

Elijah Muhammad is revered as one of the most influential black leaders of the civil rights movement. He wrote several books, including *Eat to Live,* which has sold millions of copies. He was an accomplished traveler, and he established liaisons with several major Islamic countries before his death. Despite his unorthodox teachings, he was accepted and acknowledged throughout the worldwide Islamic community.

After Elijah Muhammad's death in 1975, his son and successor Warith Deen Muhammad attempted to redirect the doctrinal teachings of the organization in the direction of Orthodox Islam. This caused great controversy, and in 1977 Minister Louis Farrakhan split with Warith Deen Muhammad and continued the teachings of Elijah Muhammad.[9] Warith Deen Muhammad established the World Community of Al-Islam in the West (later the American Muslim Mission). Almost twenty-five years after their split, Minister Farrakhan and Warith Deen Muhammad reconciled at the Nation of Islam's 2000 Savior's Day Celebration. Minister Farrakhan said in his address, "Imam [Warith Deen Muhammad] and I will be together until death overtakes us, and we will work together for the cause of Islam. We will work together for the establishment of Islam, not only among our people, but to establish Islam in the Americas."[10]

WHAT SOCIAL FACTORS LED TO THE EMERGENCE OF THE BLACK ISLAM MOVEMENT?

The philosophical distinction between black Christianity and black Islam became apparent during the 1950s and '60s when the time arose to adopt a collective strategy for fighting racial terrorism. Christian leaders such as Dr. Martin Luther King Jr. promoted nonviolence as a strategy for social change. The nonviolent, or passive resistance, movement led by Dr. King received its spiritual inspiration from the examples set by Jesus Christ. Dr. King claims that his political inspiration came from the East Indian revolutionary Gandhi. Ironically, Gandhi's nonviolent strategy was influenced by the South African struggle to which he was exposed before returning to India.

While the majority of black Christian leaders did not consider violence to be a useful means to achieve equal rights, even in the wake of violent attacks by lynch mobs and the Ku Klux Klan, the notion of a revolution by force was looming on the horizon. As blacks intensified their efforts of nonviolent protest and voter registration, whites intensified the violence—the situation reaching its peak when four little girls were killed in a church bombing in Birmingham, Alabama, and a whole group of people was attacked in Selma, Alabama. In addition, the nationwide protest of the Vietnam War added to the civil unrest. The persistence of violence on the part of the federal government and angry whites gave credence to the apocalyptic predictions of the emerging Islamic leader Elijah Muhammad.

Elijah (Poole) Muhammad, the founder of the Nation of Islam, emerged at a time when the reality of a race war was becoming more imminent. But Muhammad's philosophy was not one of a bloody jihad. Rather, his ideas encompassed an internal or spiritual jihad by which blacks could find knowledge of self. The Nation of Islam began an intense recruiting campaign in which they solicited membership and passed out literature in nightclubs as well as in church parking lots after Sunday worship services. While King, the dominant figure in the eyes of the media, maintained his position of nonviolence, he lived every waking moment with full understanding of the growing influence of the black nationalist and black Islamic movements. Sadly, the nonviolent civil rights movement died along with King—and the black Islamic movement moved into the forefront with an intensive social and economic plan.

WHAT IS THE UNIQUE APPEAL OF ISLAM FOR BLACKS?

With the dawn of the Pan-African movement during the late nineteenth century, African and Negro scholars noticed that Negro people had no recognized place of honor within the halls of traditional European Christendom; neither were the scholarly contributions of African and Negro theologians mentioned by mainstream white preachers. Historically, the bulk of theology surrounding Negroes was limited to their "place" in the human family and in the American social order. In fact, many Christian scholars believed that slavery was worthy because it civilized Negroes and provided them a means of escaping extinction.

But Islam considered Negroes to be equal and not subordinate to other races of the world. The words of the prophet Muhammad granted Africans a position of honor and placed them as equals among the holy men of Islam: "I admonish you to fear God and yield obedience to my successor, although he may be a black slave."[11] Also, many of Prophet Muhammad's officers and confidants were African. To some, this fact made Islam far more appealing than Christianity, which endorsed the slave trade and was used as a tool of oppression and divisiveness rather than unity.

Back in 1946 Dr. Buell Gallagher, who was president of the City College of New York, made this interesting observation: "There are signs that the Pan-Islamic movement may harden into a new political nationalism, based on race, which may replace the Islam of an international and interracial brotherhood. This Pan-Islamic spirit which appears about to come to full fruition in a union of the entire Muslim world against the rest of the globe is one of tomorrow's imponderables."[12]

WHY IS THE MESSAGE OF ISLAM APPEALING TO AFRICAN-AMERICAN MALES IN PARTICULAR?

The Nation of Islam promotes a social philosophy that best represents the moral and spiritual needs of African-American men. According to men I've talked to, the Nation of Islam provides a sense of belonging and self-worth distinct from the traditional stigma placed on black men, and it also gives black males a forum for challenging the paradox of American social order. While black Christian churches have tried to work with the government and create networks with other organizations, black Muslims have promoted a philosophy of self-help, tending to challenge the government and all things considered American. Examples include Mahmoud Abdul-Rauf, who refused to stand during the playing of the national anthem at a National Basketball Association game, and Muhammad Ali, who refused to join the United States armed forces. Daniel Pipes, director of The Middle East Forum, a think tank, recounted the anti-American sentiments of Abdul-Rauf, a former black Baptist minister who converted to Islam:

> A black, twenty-seven-year-old former Baptist from Mississippi who had converted to Islam in 1991, [Abdul-Rauf] declared that as a Muslim, he could not pay homage to the American flag—which he called a "symbol of oppression, of tyranny." He argued further that the flag directly contradicted his Islamic faith: "This country has a long history of [oppression]. I don't think you can argue the facts. You can't be for God and for oppression. It's clear in the Koran. Islam is the only way."[13]

The single most significant event in the history of the black Muslim movement was the Million-Man March, which called for African-American men to unify and "atone" for previous sins against the community. It was a rallying call for black men to take their place in society and repent for neglecting their duty. But the march also proved to be a great opportunity for Minister Farrakhan to receive national attention and promote the message of Islam. This event was sponsored primarily by the Nation of Islam but included the support of thousands of Christians attracted by the themes of atonement and self-identity. While some critics claimed that the march was more of an Islamic show of force, Minister Farrakhan was able to unite the diverse sectors of African-American personality.

The Nation of Islam has penetrated prison walls, seemingly working miracles with the most hardened criminals. This is typified by the life of the movement's most charismatic leader, Malcolm Little, who converted to Islam while in prison and changed his name to Malcolm X. The security arm of the Nation of Islam—the Fruit of Islam—has been responsible for reducing crime in certain inner-city Chicago communities by 80 percent and in some areas has developed an entire block into an economic center.

Black Islam, and in particular the Nation of Islam, has recruited men of distinction, from former world heavyweight boxing champions Muhammad Ali and Mike Tyson, to the former head of the NAACP, Ben Chavis (now Benjamin Muhammad). All who have their hand on the pulse of the African-American community can attest to the overwhelming success of the Nation of Islam as a social and community organization.

WHO WAS MALCOLM X?

The most popular and influential Muslim of African-American descent was El-Hajj Malik al-Shabazz, better known as Malcolm X. Not only has his life been the topic of much debate among the world's intellectual community, but he is recognized by both Muslims and Christians as being one of the greatest leaders of his time. Malcolm X chose to wage his struggle over the issue of human rights and dignity for the black man and demanded that America be indicted for its treatment of its African-American population. His background, his issue, and his solution were important because he came from the time-honored tradition of righteous men who stood firm against oppression.

The departure of Malcolm X from the Nation of Islam in March of 1964 brought much attention to the personal life of Elijah Muhammad and the legitimacy of the Nation of Islam as an organization. While Malcolm X had been responsible for much of the Nation of Islam's success after he left prison as a convert to the Nation of Islam in 1952, he was soon disenchanted when some of Elijah Muhammad's staff revealed that Elijah Muhammad had allegedly fathered several illegitimate children. This information was devastating to Malcolm X and in his eyes seemed to disqualify Elijah Muhammad from really being a prophet of Allah.

Malcolm X later discovered on his pilgrimage to Mecca that the Islamic world was comprised of diverse ethnic groups, including Caucasians—a revelation that caused a shift in his philosophy—and he soon parted ways with his mentor and started his own organization. Despite the rhetoric of the Nation's leaders, the bulk of violence perpetrated by its members has been directed against excommunicated members. It has been alleged that the Nation of Islam assassinated Malcolm X in 1965, but this allegation hasn't been proven in a court of law.

IS ISLAM BECOMING THE TRUE RELIGION OF THE BLACK MAN?

Elijah Muhammad once said, "With the help of Allah, these two opponents of Islam [Christianity and Buddhism] will be so completely eradicated from the planet Earth that you won't even find a trace of them." He added, "Allah in the judgment of the world will not recognize any religion other than Islam."[14] While the Nation of Islam has done a good job of appealing to the "blackness" of African-American people, recent numbers estimate that African-American Muslims, which make up more than 30 percent of the American Islamic population, are overwhelmingly Sunni. Even within the ranks of the black Islamic fringe, the trend is toward orthodox Islam at some point. Muslim populations in America have risen significantly in the past ten years and have seen a startling number of whites convert to Islam from Christianity as well. The manifest success of Islam in previously Christian countries like Indonesia and Egypt gives further credence to the viability of the system of Islam in acts of national liberation. Investigations after the September 11, 2001, terrorist attack have revealed that a significant portion of the world's Islamic community is either African or African-American. According to an article published in *Christianity Today,* of the majority of Americans that converted to Islam, 85 to 90 percent were African-American.[15] According to Carl Ellis, an expert on black Islam, one out of every fifteen blacks identifies himself or herself as Muslim, and there are approximately 2.6 million African-American Muslims in America.[16]

DO BLACK MUSLIMS HAVE MISPERCEPTIONS ABOUT THE CHRISTIAN FAITH?

The misconceptions that black Muslims have about Christ are similar to those of orthodox Muslims. First, a Christian must be able to prove that Christianity is not a white man's religion. A Christian should be prepared to defend the inerrancy of the Bible, the deity of Christ, and the supremacy of Christ. A Christian who witnesses to a black Muslim should be prepared for a lengthy dialogue but should also feel comfortable, because black Muslims have been taught to be respectful and tactful. They have a useful familiarity with the Bible and will often make reference to specific Scriptures. The Christian should also be able to highlight those Bible verses and passages that represent the universality of the gospel message. Finally, a Christian's motivation for approaching black Muslims must be to *make friends* rather than simply to win a theological debate. In order to effectively witness about Jesus Christ to black Muslims, a Christian must be willing to be changed by the relationship to the same degree that a Christian expects a black Muslim to be changed by adopting the Christian faith. In the exchange of ideas with Muslims, the Christian becomes more aware of the rudiments of the world and the Muslim gains the saving knowledge of Jesus Christ. I have never seen a black Muslim accept Jesus Christ from one encounter. However, some of the most dedicated Christians I know have been saved out of the Nation of Islam.

DOES BLACK ISLAM RECOGNIZE THE DEITY OF JESUS CHRIST?

When discussing Jesus Christ, the black Islamic movement asserts claims that are similar to orthodox Islam. To the black Muslim, Jesus was a prophet but was by no means divine and did not die on a cross. Using the Holy Qur'an Sharrieff (translated into English by Maulvi Muhammad Ali), the Nation of Islam has developed a different account of the crucifixion of Jesus. Note the words of Elijah Muhammad: "No one after death has ever gone any place but where they were carried. There is no heaven or hell other than on earth for you and me, and Jesus was no exception. His body is still in Palestine and will remain there."[17]

According to Elijah Muhammad, black people should not recognize the deity of Christ, the virgin birth, the immutability of the Bible, or the claims of the New Testament. Elijah Muhammad claims that the Bible, especially the King James Version, is "poison" and a hoax designed to deceive

God's chosen people. He also claims that the term *Christianity* was concocted by the very people who hated Jesus and that Jesus' teachings were actually Islam. Finally, Elijah Muhammad claims that the birth of Jesus to Mary was a sign to the Jews but did not extend to the world. He states that Jesus did not die on a literal cross but was killed with a sword as he stretched forth his hands, like a cross.[18] The position of Elijah Muhammad regarding Jesus is found in one of his most popular and controversial works, *The History of Jesus' Birth, Death and What It Means to You and Me.*

SHOULD BLACK MUSLIMS BE ALLOWED TO SPEAK IN BLACK CHURCHES?

Although Minister Farrakhan has been invited to speak at many black churches about civil rights issues, some black Christians see his acceptance into the pulpit as a contradiction and compromise of the gospel. Since Minister Farrakhan has apologized for his anti-Semitic rhetoric, most black Christians will tolerate his ideas on politics and race relations. But his belief as a Muslim is that Jesus Christ was not divine. In Sura 4:171 the Qur'an says, "Glory be to [Allah]; (far exalted is He) above having a son. To [Allah] belong all things in the heavens and on earth." The Qur'an also teaches that Jesus Christ was not crucified, nor did he die on a literal cross. Sura 4:156 says, "They did not slay him, neither crucified him, only a likeness of that was shown to them."

The Bible gives clear instructions on how to recognize those who do not believe in the deity of Christ.

> Dear friends, do not believe every spirit, but test the spirits to see whether they are from God, because many false prophets have gone out into the world. This is how you can recognize the Spirit of God: Every spirit that acknowledges that Jesus Christ has come in the flesh is from God, but every spirit that does not acknowledge Jesus is not from God. This is the spirit of the antichrist, which you have heard is coming and even now is already in the world. . . .

> This is how God showed his love among us: He sent his one and only Son into the world that we might live through him. . . .

And we have seen and testify that the Father has sent his Son to
be the Savior of the world. If anyone acknowledges that Jesus is the
Son of God, God lives in him and he in God.

1 John 4:1–3, 9, 14–15

The biblical truth mentioned here disqualifies Minister Farrakhan or
any other non-Christian from being eligible to speak in the place of the
gospel preacher, regardless of the topic. The pulpit of the church is a sacred
place where eternal, absolute truth is articulated to humankind and should
not be used to promote personal ideas and political propaganda. The pulpit is where Christ speaks, and there is no room for those who speak other
doctrines. So the question is not whether Minister Farrakhan should be
able to speak in the pulpit but whether churches will succumb to outside
political pressures. While any political or historic speech is subject to debate,
the truth of Christ is nondebatable and should not be compromised.

The Word of God and the truth of Christ are not subject to taking a
backseat to the political relevance of any person. Minister Farrakhan does
not neglect his religion, and this is clear, because he opens every speech
with "I greet you in the Name of Allah, The Beneficent, the Merciful." In
fact, the Qur'an warns Muslims not to associate with Christians. Sura 5:56
says, "O believers, take not Jews and Christians as friends; they are friends
of each other. Whoso of you makes them his friends is one of them. God
guides not the people of the evildoers."

If Minister Farrakhan's intentions are true to Islam, his ultimate goal is
to spread Islam and not simply fight for the cause of civil rights. Many
people are attracted to the Nation of Islam because of its use of Christian
genre and its manifest success in the black community. But upon examina-
tion of the context, it soon becomes apparent that Minister Farrakhan and
other black Muslims had significant contact with the church during their
early years but now exhibit an inaccurate understanding of the Christian
faith, which they use to seduce unsuspecting people, many of whom were
Christians of African descent.

It is Satan's goal to exploit the longings of people and entice Christians
into darkness through craftiness and sensationalism. Satan also gains employ-

ment through our ignorance, emotions, and even our passions. Christians should remember that the ties they have with Jesus Christ run far deeper than those of race, kinship, or political affiliation (see Matthew 10:37). Jesus commands his church to be a light to the community (see Matthew 5:14–16) and stay faithful to their beliefs (see Revelation 2–3). No matter how well a person articulates a message, the truth of the message is subject to the assertions of Jesus Christ. Christ's death was the greatest act of love and created the strongest degree of unity within the broadest field of diversity. His sacrifice awarded the highest medal of honor to the lowliest of people.

HOW MIGHT THE CHURCH REACH OUT TO BLACK MUSLIMS?

The first church was not without its share of racial strife. But the problem of race was solved by providing the group with stewards who were able to minister to diverse groups of people. These were sensitive men who were used by the Holy Spirit to administer equity among the church members. There was no remedy for the rift between the Jew and the Greek except equity. The same is required considering the dismal state of affairs among black and white Christians.

Before the church can reach black Muslims, the church must first seek to mend the rift that exists between black and white Christians in America. This cannot happen until blacks and whites share the same needs. The need for black organizations such as the Nation of Islam and the Black Panther party will persist until white churches consider racism, poverty, and miseducation to be just as important as abortion and homosexuality. White churches must seek to establish healthy relationships with black churches whereby both groups can learn from each other rather than one group being the mere benefactor of the other's services. This would establish a precedent within the community for building relationships with other non–Christian organizations as well. Once black and white churches have buried the hatchet of divisiveness, they must collectively engage local Islamic organizations in dialogue about the problems of race and make a good-faith effort to assist in the rebuilding of the black community. Reconciliation is not a onetime event but is an attempt to create a new culture, a counterculture of sorts, divorced from the divisions created by the previous social order.

It is not necessary that one be an apologist per se to witness to black Muslims. But one must be willing to adopt the needs of others as their own and to suffer as those whom he or she seeks to win to Christ. Apologetics is a battle of arguments, and it is possible for a trained theologian to win the intellectual battle and lose the war, which is to introduce the Muslim to Jesus Christ. When witnessing to black Muslims, it is unproductive to criticize Minister Farrakhan or other Islamic leaders or to dispute historical facts. But it is necessary to commit to memory some aspects of the black Islamic philosophy and show how these philosophies contradict the Bible. Also, Christians must seek to emphasize those Scriptures that command racial parity within the church and should be able to respond to the lack of parity in today's church. Finally, the Christian must pray that the mind of the Muslim be opened to receive the gospel.

Conclusion

The early Islamic presence in America created the social consciousness that would be the catalyst for what is now referred to by some as "Black Islam." The early movement merged the teachings of Islam with the ethos of the struggle for black independence. The efforts of the early black Muslims are important because they gave birth to several personalities who were some of the most influential Muslims in the world. Most notably, from the roots of the early black Muslims would come the most significant and influential black organization in America—the Nation of Islam.

America is a land of categories and distinctions that Jesus considered unimportant. As long as Sunday morning remains the most segregated hour of the week, the American church will continue to see casualties among its population. American Christians are called to accept the ministry of reconciliation and seek to mend the cultural divide that threatens to render the church ineffective.

Questions for Reflection and Discussion

1. Are racial or ethnic ties stronger than religious commitments? Why or why not? Should these ties outweigh one's religious identity, or is there no legitimate need to distinguish religion in terms of *black* and *white?*

2. Are black churches doing enough to develop and positively influence the black community?

3. Considering the many ethnic conflicts around the world and the continued racial strife in America, how might American Christians distinctly model the love of Christ and racial reconciliation in their own churches and neighborhoods?

RESOURCES FOR DIGGING DEEPER

CHAPTER 1: TOUGH QUESTIONS ABOUT GOD

Geisler, Norman L. "God." *Baker Encyclopedia of Christian Apologetics.*
Grand Rapids: Baker, 1999.

Geisler, Norman L., and Ronald M. Brooks. *When Skeptics Ask:*
A Handbook of Christian Evidences. Grand Rapids: Baker, 1995.

http://www.impactapologetics.com

http://www.normgeisler.com

CHAPTER 2: TOUGH QUESTIONS ABOUT EVIL

Geisler, Norman L. "Evil." *Baker Encyclopedia of Christian Apologetics.* Grand
Rapids: Baker, 1999.

_____. "God and the Problem of Evil," "If God, Why Evil?" "The
Problem of Evil," "What about Evil?" audiotapes available for purchase
at the Norman Geisler website: http://www.normgeisler.com

_____. *Philosophy of Religion.* Grand Rapids: Baker, 1988. This book is
out of print, but a bound copy of the book is available for purchase
at the Norman Geisler website: http://www.normgeisler.com

_____. *The Roots of Evil.* Dallas: Probe, 1989. This book is out of print,
but a bound copy of the book is available for purchase at the
Norman Geisler website: http://www.normgeisler.com

Geisler, Norman L., and Ronald M. Brooks. "Questions about Evil."
Chapter 4 in *When Skeptics Ask.* Grand Rapids: Baker, 1995.

Habermas, Gary. "Atheism and Evil: A Fatal Dilemma," audiotape
available for purchase at Norman Geisler website:
http://www.normgeisler.com

Lewis, C. S. *A Grief Observed*. Reprint edition. San Francisco: HarperSanFrancisco, 2001.

_____. *The Problem of Pain*. Reprint edition. San Francisco: HarperSanFrancisco, 2001.

Rhodes, Ron. "Is Evil an Apologetic against Christianity?" audiotape available from the Ron Rhodes website: http://www.ronrhodes.org

Rood, Rick. "The Problem of Evil: How Can a Good God Allow Evil?" 1996. Probe Ministries website: http://www.probe.org

Story, Dan. *Defending Your Faith*. Nashville: Nelson, 1992.

Yancey, Philip. *Disappointment with God*. Grand Rapids: Zondervan, 1997.

_____. *Where Is God When It Hurts?* Grand Rapids: Zondervan, 2001.

CHAPTER 3: TOUGH QUESTIONS ABOUT SCIENCE

Behe, Michael. *Darwin's Black Box*. New York: Free Press, 1996.

Denton, Michel. *Evolution: A Theory in Crisis*. Bethesda, Md.: Adler & Adler, 1985.

Johnson, Phillip E. *Darwin on Trial*. Downer's Grove, Ill.: InterVarsity Press, 1991.

Thaxton, Charles B., Walter L. Bradley, and Roger Olsen. *The Mystery of Life's Origin*. New York: Philosophical Library, 1984.

Thaxton, Charles B., and Nancy R. Pearcey. *The Soul of Science*. Wheaton, Ill.: Crossway, 1994.

White, Andrew Dickson. *A History of the Warfare of Science with Theology in Christendom*. 2 vols. Reprint edition. Maclean, Va.: IndyPublish.com, 2002.

CHAPTERS 4 AND 5: TOUGH QUESTIONS ABOUT CHRIST

Copan, Paul, ed. *Will the Real Jesus Please Stand Up: A Debate Between William Lane Craig and John Dominic Crossan*. Grand Rapids: Baker, 1999.

Craig, William Lane. *Reasonable Faith*. Revised edition. Page 251. Wheaton, Ill.: Crossway, 1994.

_____. *The Son Rises: Historical Evidence for the Resurrection of Jesus*. Page 140. Chicago: Moody Press, 1981.

Greenleaf, Simon. *The Testimony of the Evangelists*. Grand Rapids: Baker, 1994.

Habermas, Gary. *The Verdict of History*. Nashville: Nelson, 1988.

Kreeft, Peter, and Ronald K. Tacelli. *Handbook of Christian Apologetics*. Pages 48–88. Downers Grove, Ill.: InterVarsity Press, 1994.

Moreland, J. P. *Scaling the Secular City*. Pages 152–53. Grand Rapids: Baker, 1987.

Strobel, Lee. *The Case for Christ*. Grand Rapids: Zondervan, 1998.

_____. *The Case for Faith*. Grand Rapids: Zondervan, 2000.

Wilkins, Michael J., and J. P. Moreland, gen. eds. *Jesus Under Fire: Modern Scholarship Reinvents the Historical Jesus*. Grand Rapids: Zondervan, 1995.

CHAPTERS 6 AND 7: TOUGH QUESTIONS ABOUT THE BIBLE

Blomberg, Craig L. *The Historical Reliability of the Gospels*. Downers Grove, Ill.: InterVarsity Press, 1987.

Bruce, F. F. *The New Testament Documents: Are They Reliable?* Downers Grove, Ill.: InterVarsity Press, 1984.

Geisler, Norman L., ed. *Inerrancy*. Grand Rapids: Zondervan, 2001.

Geisler, Norman L., and Thomas Howe. *When Critics Ask: A Popular Handbook on Bible Difficulties*. Grand Rapids: Baker, 1999.

Geisler, Norman L., and William E. Nix. *From God to Us: How We Got Our Bible*. Chicago: Moody Press, 1974.

_____. *A General Introduction to the Bible*. Revised and expanded. Chicago: Moody Press, 1986.

Mateen, Elas. *Understanding the Koran: A Quick Christian Guide to the Muslim Holy Book*. Grand Rapids: Zondervan, 2003.

Youngblood, Thomas L., and Sandra P. Aldrich. *The Bible Encounters: 21 Stories of Changed Lives.* Grand Rapids: Zondervan, 2002.

CHAPTERS 8 AND 9: TOUGH QUESTIONS ABOUT EASTERN RELIGIONS AND PRACTICES

Clark, David K., and Norman L. Geisler. *Apologetics in the New Age: A Christian Critique of Pantheism.* Grand Rapids: Baker, 1990.

Geisler, Norman L. *False Gods of Our Time.* Eugene, Ore.: Harvest House, 1985.

Groothuis, Douglas R. *Confronting the New Age.* Downers Grove, Ill.: InterVarsity Press, 1988.

_____. *Revealing the New Age Jesus.* Downers Grove, Ill.: InterVarsity Press, 1990.

_____. *Unmasking the New Age.* Downers Grove, Ill.: InterVarsity Press, 1986.

Guinness, Os. *The Dust of Death: The Sixties Counterculture and How It Changed America Forever,* revised edition. Wheaton, Ill.: Crossway, 1994.

Humphreys, Christmas. *The Buddhist Way of Life.* New Delhi: HarperCollins, 1993.

Johnson, David L. *A Reasoned Look at Asian Religions.* Minneapolis: Bethany House, 1985.

Langley, Myrtle. *World Religions.* Reprint edition. Wheaton, Ill.: Chariot/Victor, 1993.

Lewis, C. S. *Mere Christianity.* Reprint edition. San Francisco: HarperSanFrancisco, 2001.

_____. *The Problem of Pain.* Reprint edition. San Francisco: HarperSanFrancisco, 2001.

Mangalwadi, Vishal. *When the New Age Gets Old.* Second edition. Downers Grove, Ill.: InterVarsity Press, 1992.

McDowell, Josh, and Don Stewart. *Handbook of Today's Religions.*
    Nashville: Nelson, 1983.
Miller, Elliot. *A Crash Course on the New Age Movement.* Grand Rapids:
    Baker, 1993.
Reisser, Paul C., Teri K. Reisser, and John Weldon. *New Age Medicine.*
    Downers Grove, Ill.: InterVarsity Press, 1987.
Rhodes, Ron. *The Challenge of the Cults and New Religions.* Grand
    Rapids: Zondervan, 2001.
Schaeffer, Francis A. *Complete Works.* 5 vols. Second edition. Wheaton, Ill.:
    Crossway, 1985.

CHAPTER 10: TOUGH QUESTIONS ABOUT BLACK ISLAM

Blyden, Edward. *Christianity, Islam and the Negro Race.* Baltimore, Md.:
    Black Classic Press, 1994.
Cleaver, Eldridge. *Soul on Ice.* New York: Delta Trade Paperbacks, 1991.
Cone, James. *God of the Oppressed.* Maryknoll, N.Y.: Orbis, 1997.
Diop, Cheikh Anta. *Pre-Colonial Black Africa: A Comparative Study of the
    Political and Social Systems of Europe and Black Africa, from Antiquity to
    the Formation of Modern States.* Westport, Conn.: L. Hill, 1987.
Felder, Cain Hope. *Stony the Road We Trod: African American Biblical
    Interpretation.* Minneapolis: Fortress, 1991.
Friedly, Michael. *Malcolm X: The Assassination.* New York: Carroll &
    Graf / R. Gallen, 1992.
Galli, Mark. "Bound for Canaan: The Spiritual Journey of Africans in
    America 1619–1865." *Christian History* 62 (1999): 10–46.
George, Timothy. *Is the Father of Jesus the God of Muhammad?* Grand
    Rapids: Zondervan, 2002.
Jaaber, Heshaam. *The Final Chapter: I Buried Malcolm.* Jersey City, N.J.:
    New Mind Productions, 1993.
Johnson, Paul. *African American Christianity: Essays in History.* Berkeley:
    University of California Press, 1994.

Lee, Martha. *The Nation of Islam: An American Millenarian Movement.*
Syracuse, N.Y.: Syracuse University Press, 1996.

Muhammad, Elijah. *Message to the Black Man in America.* Atlanta:
Messenger Elijah Muhammad Propagation Society, 1997.

_____. *The Supreme Wisdom: Solution to the So-Called Negroes' Problem.*
Chicago: University of Islam, 1957.

Contacts:

Rev. Carl Ellis, Project Joseph, Chattanooga, Tennessee. Contact Project
Joseph at P.O. Box 16616, Chattanooga, TN 37416. Phone:
423-490-9194.

Rev. Robert White, Central Community Christian Church,
Montgomery, Alabama. Contact the church at 981 S. Perry Street,
Montgomery, AL 36104. Phone: 334-269-0457.

NOTES

Chapter 1.
Tough Questions about God

1. Of course, the actual amount of energy remains constant; only the usable amount is decreasing.
2. Robert Jastrow, *God and the Astronomers* (New York: W. W. Norton, 1978), 15–16.
3. David Hume, *The Letters of David Hume,* vol. 1, ed. J. Y. T. Greig (Oxford: Clarendon, 1932), 187.
4. David Hume, *Enquiry Concerning Human Understanding,* ed. Chas. W. Hendel (New York: Liberal Arts, 1955), 165–66.
5. C. S. Lewis, *The Abolition of Man* (New York: Macmillan, 1947), 69.
6. C. S. Lewis, *The Problem of Pain* (New York: HarperCollins, 2001, reprint; first published, 1944), 120.

Chapter 2.
Tough Questions about Evil

1. Cited by Lee Strobel, "Why Does God Allow Suffering?" (message delivered at Saddleback Valley Community Church, El Toro, California, 26 February 2000).
2. Ken Boa and Larry Moody, *I'm Glad You Asked* (Colorado Springs: Victor, 1994), 129.
3. Norman L. Geisler, *Baker Encyclopedia of Christian Apologetics* (Grand Rapids: Baker, 1999), 220.
4. Geisler, *Baker Encyclopedia of Christian Apologetics,* 220.
5. Millard J. Erickson, *Introducing Christian Doctrine* (Grand Rapids: Baker, 1996), 138–39.

6. Erickson, *Introducing Christian Doctrine,* 139.

7. Norman L. Geisler and Ronald M. Brooks, *When Skeptics Ask* (Wheaton, Ill.:Victor, 1990), 59–60.

8. Boa and Moody, *I'm Glad You Asked,* 122.

9. Cited in Erickson, *Introducing Christian Doctrine,* 138–39.

10. Robert Morey, *The New Atheism and the Erosion of Freedom* (Minneapolis: Bethany House, 1986), 153.

11. Morey, *The New Atheism,* 153.

12. Paul E. Little, *Know Why You Believe* (Downers Grove, Ill.: InterVarsity Press, 1975), 81.

13. Little, *Know Why You Believe,* 81.

14. Geisler and Brooks, *When Skeptics Ask,* 73.

15. Cited in Little, *Know Why You Believe,* 87.

16. Boa and Moody, *I'm Glad You Asked,* 131.

17. Norman L. Geisler and Jeff Amanu, "Evil," in *New Dictionary of Theology,* ed. Sinclair B. Ferguson and David F. Wright (Downers Grove, Ill.: InterVarsity Press, 1988), 242.

18. Rick Rood, "The Problem of Evil: How Can a Good God Allow Evil?" (1996), Probe Ministries website: http://www.probe.org

19. Boa and Moody, *I'm Glad You Asked,* 133.

20. Cited in Dan Story, *Defending Your Faith* (Nashville: Nelson, 1992), 171–72.

21. Geisler and Brooks, *When Skeptics Ask,* 73.

22. Geisler and Brooks, *When Skeptics Ask,* 64–65.

23. Little, *Know Why You Believe,* 81.

24. Story, *Defending Your Faith,* 176–77.

25. Harold Kushner, *When Bad Things Happen to Good People* (New York: Schocken, 1981), 134.

26. Kushner, *When Bad Things Happen,* 43.

27. Boa and Moody, *I'm Glad You Asked,* 127.

28. Mary Baker Eddy, *Miscellaneous Writings* (Boston: Christian Science Publishing Society, 1896), 27.

29. Emily Cady, *Lessons in Truth* (Kansas City, Mo.: Unity School of Christianity, 1941), 35.

30. Ernest Holmes, *What Religious Science Teaches* (Los Angeles: Science of Mind Publications, 1974), 13.

31. Walter Martin, *The Kingdom of the Cults* (Minneapolis: Bethany House, 1997), 40–41.

32. David Spangler, *Revelation: The Birth of a New Age* (Middleton, Wis.: Lorian, 1976), 13.

33. Rabi Maharaj, "Death of a Guru: The Personal Testimony of Rabi Maharaj," *Christian Research Newsletter* 3, no. 3 (1990), 2.

34. David Gershon and Gail Straub, *Empowerment: The Art of Creating Your Life as You Want It* (New York: Delta, 1989), 35.

35. Gershon and Straub, *Empowerment,* 36.

36. Shirley MacLaine, cited in Douglas Groothuis, "A Summary Critique," book review of *It's All in the Playing,* in *Christian Research Journal* (Fall 1987): 28.

37. Cited in Douglas Groothuis, "A Summary Critique," 28.

38. Gary Zukav, *The Seat of the Soul* (New York: Simon and Schuster, 1989), 45.

39. See Norman L. Geisler, *The Root of Evil* (Dallas: Probe, 1989); C. S. Lewis, *The Great Divorce* (New York: Macmillan, 1946); and C. S. Lewis, *The Problem of Pain* (New York: HarperCollins, 2001, reprint; first published, 1940).

40. Geisler and Amanu, "Evil," 242.

41. Geisler, *Baker Encyclopedia of Christian Apologetics,* 222.

42. Erickson, *Introducing Christian Doctrine,* 141–42.

43. Gary R. Habermas and J. P. Moreland, *Immortality: The Other Side of Death* (Nashville: Nelson, 1992), 185.

Chapter 3.
Tough Questions about Science

1. Andrew Dickson White, *A History of the Warfare of Science with Theology in Christendom,* 2 vols., reprint ed. (New York: Dover, 1960).

2. Charles B. Thaxton and Nancy R. Pearcey, *The Soul of Science* (Wheaton, Ill.: Crossway, 1994).

3. Loren Eiseley, "Francis Bacon," in *The Horizon Book of Makers of Modern Thought* (New York: American Heritage, 1972), 95–96.

4. Loren Eiseley, *Darwin's Century* (Garden City, N.Y.: Doubleday, 1961), 62.

5. Freeman J. Dyson, "Is God in the Lab?" *The New York Review of Books,* 28 May 1998, 8.

6. C. P. Snow, "The Two Cultures," in *The Two Cultures and a Second Look* (Cambridge: Cambridge University Press, 1969).

7. Victor Weisskopf, "Frontiers and Limits of Science," *Alexander von Humboldt Stiftung: Mitteilungen* 43 (March 1984): 1–11; cf. a similar paper by the same author in *American Scientist* 65 (1977): 405.

8. John Barrow and Frank Tipler, *The Anthropic Cosmological Principle* (Oxford: Clarendon, 1986), 442.

9. Quentin Smith, "The Uncaused Beginning of the Universe," in William Lane Craig and Quentin Smith, *Theism, Atheism, and Big Bang Cosmology* (Oxford: Clarendon, 1993), 120.

10. Arthur Eddington, *The Expanding Universe* (New York: Macmillan, 1933), 124.

11. Eddington, *The Expanding Universe,* 178.

12. For discussion see my "Naturalism and Cosmology," in *Naturalism: A Critical Appraisal*, ed. Wm. L. Craig and J. P. Moreland, Routledge Studies in Twentieth-Century Philosophy (London: Routledge, 2000), 215–52.

13. Stephen Hawking, *A Brief History of Time* (New York: Bantam, 1988), 140–41.

14. Arthur Eddington, *Space, Time, and Gravitation,* reprint. ed. (Cambridge: Cambridge University Press, 1987), 48.

15. Eddington, *Space, Time, and Gravitation,* 181.

16. Stephen Hawking and Roger Penrose, *The Nature of Space and Time,* The Isaac Newton Institute Series of Lectures (Princeton, N.J.: Princeton University Press, 1996), 3–4, 121.

17. See John D. Barrow, *Theories of Everything* (Oxford: Clarendon, 1991), 67–68.

18. Hawking and Penrose, *The Nature of Space and Time,* 20.

19. Andrei Linde, who thinks that Steinhardt's model "is plagued by numerous unsolved problems," complains that the cyclic/ekpyrotic scenario is "very popular among journalists" but "rather unpopular among scientists" ("Cyclic Universe Runs into Criticism," *Physics World* [June 2002], 8).

20. J. M. Wersinger, "Genesis: The Origin of the Universe," *National Forum* (winter 1996), 9, 12. Wersinger himself apparently tries to avoid the absolute origin of the universe from nothing by appeal to a vacuum fluctuation, an idea that has been shown untenable, as I explain in the article referred to in note 19.

21. John Barrow, *The World Within the World* (Oxford: Clarendon, 1988).

22. Paul Davies, "God and Time Machines," *Books and Culture* (March/April 2002), 29.

23.   John C. Polkinghorne, *Serious Talk: Science and Religion in Dialogue* (London: SCM Press, 1996), 6.

24.   I owe this insight to the philosopher of science Robin Collins.

25.   Ludwig Boltzmann, *Lectures on Gas Theory,* trans. Stephen G. Brush (Berkeley: University of California Press, 1964), 446–48.

26.   Fred Hoyle and Chandra Wickramasinghe, *Evolution from Space* (New York: Simon & Schuster, 1981), 24.

27.   Charles B. Thaxton, Walter L. Bradley, and Roger Olsen, *The Mystery of Life's Origin* (New York: Philosophical Library, 1984).

28.   Francis Crick, "In the Beginning...," *Scientific American* (February 1991), 125.

29.   Nathan Aviezer, *In the Beginning* (Hoboken, NJ: KTAV Publishing House, 1990).

30.   Phillip E. Johnson, *Darwin on Trial* (Downer's Grove, Ill.: InterVarsity Press, 1991). The Intelligent Design movement, whose leaders include William Dembski, Stephen Meyer, Paul Nelson, Michael Behe, and Jonathan Wells, emphasizes the need for intelligent agency behind biological complexity, while remaining neutral on issues of interventionism (creationism) and theism (God).

31.   Michael Denton, *Evolution: A Theory in Crisis* (Bethesda, Md.: Adler & Adler, 1985), chapters 8–9.

32.   Barrow and Tipler, *The Anthropic Cosmological Principle,* 561–65.

33.   Barrow and Tipler, *The Anthropic Cosmological Principle,* 133.

34.   Michael Behe, *Darwin's Black Box* (New York: Free Press, 1996).

35.   For Behe's response to critics, see Michael Behe, "The Modern Intelligent Design Hypothesis: Breaking Rules," *Philosophia Christi* 3, no. 1 (2001), 165–79.

Chapter 4.
Tough Questions about Christ

1.   For a description of the specific evidence that convinced me of Jesus' deity, see Lee Strobel, *The Case for Christ* (Grand Rapids: Zondervan, 1998), and Lee Strobel, *The Case for Faith* (Grand Rapids: Zondervan, 2000).

2.   For a more detailed discussion of their approach, see Michael J. Wilkins and J. P. Moreland, eds., *Jesus Under Fire: Modern Scholarship Reinvents the Historical Jesus* (Grand Rapids: Zondervan, 1995), especially chapters 1 and 5.

3. For a brief history of the distinction between the Jesus of history and the Christ of faith, see Norman L. Geisler, *Baker Encyclopedia of Christian Apologetics* (Grand Rapids: Baker, 1999), 141–42.

4. Richard N. Ostling, "Who was Jesus Christ?" *Time* 15 August 1988.

5. Cited in Strobel, *The Case for Christ,* 22–25.

6. Irenaeus, *Adversus haereses* 3.3.4.

7. Hank Hanegraaff, "The Search for Jesus Hoax," *Christian Research Journal* 23, no. 2 (2001), 14.

8. Cited in Strobel, *The Case for Faith,* 137, 139.

9. Simon Greenleaf, *The Testimony of the Evangelists* (Grand Rapids: Baker, 1994), vii.

10. See Strobel, *The Case for Christ,* 99.

11. Norman Geisler and Thomas Howe, *When Critics Ask* (Wheaton, Ill.: Victor, 1992), 385.

12. Cited in Strobel, *The Case for Christ,* 97.

13. Clifford Wilson, *Rocks, Relics, and Biblical Reliability* (Grand Rapids: Zondervan, 1977), 120.

14. Cited in Strobel, *The Case for Christ,* 33.

15. J. P. Moreland, *Scaling the Secular City* (Grand Rapids: Baker, 1987), 152–53.

16. Moreland, *Scaling the Secular City,* 154.

17. Moreland, *Scaling the Secular City,* 148.

18. Moreland, *Scaling the Secular City,* 149. For examples of creeds and hymns, see Romans 1:3–4; 1 Corinthians 11:23–26; 15:3–8; Philippians 2:6–11; Colossians 1:15–18; 1 Timothy 3:16; 2 Timothy 2:8.

19. Moreland, *Scaling the Secular City,* 149.

20. See A. N. Sherwin-White, *Roman Society and Roman Law in the New Testament* (Grand Rapids: Baker, 1978), 186–93.

21. Frederic Kenyon, *Handbook to the Textual Criticism of the New Testament* (New York: Macmillan, 1912), 5.

22. Frederic Kenyon, *The Bible and Archaeology* (New York: Harper, 1940), 288.

23. See Strobel, *The Case for Christ,* 38–54.

24. H. R. Macintosh, *The Person of Jesus Christ* (Edinburgh: T. & T. Clark, 1913), 2.

25. Cited in John N. Akers, John H. Armstrong, and John D. Woodbridge, gen. eds., *This We Believe* (Grand Rapids: Zondervan, 2000), 64.

26. William Lane Craig, *The Son Rises: Historical Evidence for the Resurrection of Jesus* (Chicago: Moody Press, 1981), 140.

27. Cited in Akers, Armstrong, and Woodbridge, *This We Believe,* 65.

28. See Akers, Armstrong, and Woodbridge, *This We Believe,* 64.

29. Cited in Strobel, *The Case for Christ,* 157.

30. Cited in Strobel, *The Case for Christ,* 134.

31. Cited in Strobel, *The Case for Christ,* 136.

32. Cited in Strobel, *The Case for Christ,* 137.

33. William Lane Craig, *Reasonable Faith,* rev. ed. (Wheaton, Ill.: Crossway, 1994), 251.

34. Cited in Strobel, *The Case for Christ,* 135–36.

35. James D. G. Dunn, *Jesus and the Spirit* (London: SCM Press, 1975), 60, cited in Craig, *Reasonable Faith,* 250.

36. Royce Gruenler, *New Approaches to Jesus and the Gospels* (Grand Rapids: Baker, 1982), 74.

Chapter 5.
More Tough Questions about Christ

1. John Stott, *Basic Christianity* (Downers Grove, Ill.: InterVarsity Press, 1964), 26.

2. Carl Sagan, *Cosmos* (New York: Ballantine, 1993), 4.

3. Charles Templeton, *Farewell to God* (Toronto: McClelland & Stewart, 1996), 21.

4. Richard Dawkins, "Snake Oil and Holy Water" (available at http://www.forbes.com/asap/99/1004/235.html).

5. John Dominic Crossan, *Jesus: A Revolutionary Biography* (San Francisco: HarperSanFrancisco, 1994), 95.

6. Robert W. Funk, Roy W. Hoover, and The Jesus Seminar, *The Five Gospels* (San Francisco: HarperSanFrancisco, 1993), 2.

7. For a summary of these arguments, see Norman L. Geisler, *Baker Encyclopedia of Christian Apologetics* (Grand Rapids: Baker, 1999), 276–83. For twenty arguments in favor of God's existence, see Peter Kreeft and Ronald K. Tacelli, *Handbook of Christian Apologetics* (Downers Grove, Ill.: InterVarsity Press, 1994), 48–88.

8. Geisler, *Baker Encyclopedia of Christian Apologetics,* 450.

9. Gary Habermas, *The Historical Jesus* (Joplin. Mo.: College Press, 1996).

10. R. T. France, "The Gospels as Historical Sources for Jesus, the Founder of Christianity," *Truth* 1 (1985): 86.

11. Cited in Lee Strobel, *The Case for Christ* (Grand Rapids: Zondervan, 1998), 27.

12. Cited in Lee Strobel, *The Case for Faith* (Grand Rapids: Zondervan, 2000), 68–69.

13. See Michael J. Wilkins and J. P. Moreland, eds., *Jesus Under Fire: Modern Scholarship Reinvents the Historical Jesus* (Grand Rapids: Zondervan, 1995), 129.

14. Cited in Strobel, *The Case for Faith,* 68.

15. See Wilkins and Moreland, *Jesus Under Fire,* 131.

16. See: Stephen T. Davis, "The Miracle at Cana: A Philosopher's Perspective," in David Wenham and Craig Blomberg, eds., *The Miracles of Jesus* (Sheffield: JSOT, 1986), 429, cited in Wilkins and Moreland, *Jesus Under Fire,* 131.

17. See Sanhedrin 43a.

18. Cited in Strobel, *The Case for Faith,* 136.

19. See Gary Habermas, *The Verdict of History* (Nashville: Nelson, 1988), 107.

20. The Acts of Pilate to which Justin Martyr referred is not the same as the apocryphal work by that name—a fictitious piece written centuries after Pilate lived, but which unfortunately has been cited by some well-meaning but ill-informed Christians as being authentic.

21. Templeton, *Farewell to God,* 112.

22. Cited in Strobel, *The Case for Christ,* 149.

23. Cited in Wilkins and Moreland, *Jesus Under Fire,* 133.

24. Cited in Wilkins and Moreland, *Jesus Under Fire,* 134.

25. Bertrand Russell, "What Is an Agnostic?" *Look* magazine, 3 November 1953, cited in Strobel, *The Case for Faith,* 141.

26. Cited in Strobel, *The Case for Faith,* 141.

27. Alfred Edersheim, *The Life and Times of Jesus the Messiah* (Grand Rapids: Eerdmans, 1972), 160.

28. Norman L. Geisler and Ronald M. Brooks, *When Skeptics Ask* (Wheaton, Ill.: Victor, 1990), 115.

29. Geisler, *Baker Encyclopedia of Christian Apologetics,* 611.

30. Geisler and Brooks, *When Skeptics Ask,* 114–15.

31. See Peter W. Stoner, *Science Speaks* (Chicago: Moody Press, 1969).

32. Cited in Strobel, *The Case for Christ,* 183.

33. Cited in Strobel, *The Case for Christ,* 184.

34. Cited in Strobel, *The Case for Faith,* 135.

35. Geisler, *Baker Encyclopedia of Christian Apologetics,* 615.

36. Cited in Ruth Rosen, ed., *Jewish Doctors Meet the Great Physician* (San Francisco: Purple Pomegranate, 1997), 34.

37. Gary Habermas and Antony Flew, *Did Jesus Rise from the Dead?* (San Francisco: Harper & Row, 1987), xi.

38. Cited in Ross Clifford, ed., *The Case for the Empty Tomb: Leading Lawyers Look at the Resurrection* (Claremont, Calif.: Albatross, 1991), 112.

39. Cited in William D. Edwards et al., "On the Physical Death of Jesus Christ," *Journal of the American Medical Association* (21 March 1986): 1463.

40. John A. T. Robinson, *The Human Face of God* (Philadelphia: Westminster, 1973), 131, cited by William Lane Craig in *Will the Real Jesus Please Stand Up? A Debate Between William Lane Craig and John Dominic Crossan* (Grand Rapids: Baker, 1998), 27.

41. Cited in Wilkins and Moreland, *Jesus Under Fire,* 165.

42. Cited in Strobel, *The Case for Christ,* 230.

43. John Drane, *Introducing the New Testament* (San Francisco: Harper & Row, 1986), 99.

44. See Strobel, *The Case for Christ,* 220.

45. Cited in Strobel, *The Case for Christ,* 220.

46. See Strobel, *The Case for Christ,* 234.

47. See Strobel, *The Case for Christ,* 238–40.

48. Cited in Strobel, *The Case for Christ,* 121.

49. Carl Braaten, *History and Hermeneutics,* vol. 2 of *New Directions in Theology Today,* ed. William Hordern (Philadelphia: Westminster, 1966), 78.

50. J. P. Moreland, *Scaling the Secular City* (Grand Rapids: Baker, 1987), 179–80.

51. C. F. D. Moule, *The Phenomenon of the New Testament* (London: SCM, 1967), 3.

52. Cited in John N. Akers, John H. Armstrong, and John D. Woodbridge, gen. eds., *This We Believe* (Grand Rapids: Zondervan, 2000), 108–9.

Chapter 6.
Tough Questions about the Bible

1. See Norman L. Geisler and William E. Nix , *A General Introduction to the Bible* (Chicago: Moody Press, 2000), part 1.

2. For more on inerrancy, see Norman L. Geisler, ed., *Inerrancy* (Grand Rapids: Zondervan, 1980).

3. For more, see Norman L. Geisler, *Systematic Theology* (Minneapolis: Bethany House, 2001), volume 1.

4. B. B. Warfield, *Inspiration and Authority of the Bible* (Philadelphia: Presbyterian & Reformed, 1948), 299.

5. See Norman L. Geisler and Thomas Howe, *When Critics Ask* (Grand Rapids: Baker, 1992), 15–26.

6. However, Luke could have been referring to the canonical gospels of Matthew and Mark, which could have been earlier than Luke.

7. See F. F. Bruce, *The New Testament Documents: Are They Reliable?* (Downers Grove, Ill.: InterVarsity Press, 1960); Craig Blomberg, *The Historical Reliability of the Gospels* (Downers Grove, Ill.: InterVarsity Press, 1987).

8. There were nine if one of the other eight did not write Hebrews.

9. See Colin Hemer, *The Book of Acts in the Setting of Hellenic History* (Winona Lake, Ind.: Eisenbrauns, 1990).

10. See Hemer, *The Book of Acts.*

11. See Richard N. Ostling, "Jesus Christ, Plain and Simple," *Time,* 10 January 1994, 32–33.

12. Robert Funk, "Opening Remarks," *Foundations and Facets Forum* 1, no. 1 (March 1985): 12.

13. Funk, "Opening Remarks," 7.

14. Cited in Hemer, *The Book of Acts,* 8.

15. See Edwin Yamauchi, "Easter: Myth, Hallucination, or History?" *Christianity Today,* 29 March 1974.

16. See Hemer, *The Book of Acts.*

17. See John A. T. Robinson, *Redating the New Testament* (London: SCM Press, 1976).

18. Craig L. Blomberg, *The Historical Reliability of the Gospels* (Downers Grove, Ill.: InterVarsity Press, 1987).

19. Gary Habermas, *The Historical Jesus: Ancient Evidence for the Life of Christ* (Joplin, Mo.: College Press, 1996).

20. Simon Greenleaf, *A Treatise on the Law of Evidence* (Boston: C. C. Little & J. Brown, 1842).

21. Simon Greenleaf, *The Testimony of the Evangelists* (Grand Rapids: Baker, 1984 [reprint of 1874 edition]), 53–54.

22. Greenleaf, *The Testimony of the Evangelists,* 46.

23. A. T. Robertson, *An Introduction to the Textual Criticism of the New Testament* (Nashville: Broadman, 1925), 22.

Chapter 7.
Tough Questions about the Bible, False Prophets, and the Holy Books of Other Religions

1. For a more complete discussion of the evidence that the Bible is the Word of God, see Norman L. Geisler, *Baker Encyclopedia of Christian Apologetics* (Grand Rapids: Baker, 1999), especially the many articles under "Bible, . . ."

2. See Geisler, *Baker Encyclopedia of Christian Apologetics,* "Bible, Evidence for."

3. In the context of speaking of "seventy years" (Daniel 9:2), Daniel predicted that the "Anointed One" (the Messiah) would be cut off (die) after he worked to "put an end to sin, to atone for wickedness, to bring in everlasting righteousness, to seal up vision and prophecy" (verse 24). The time of this was to be 483 years after the command to rebuild Jerusalem (given in 445/444 B.C.). But these are Jewish lunar years of 360 days (12 months times 30 days a month). So, by multiplying the five extra days per year times 483, one gets more than six years on top of the 477 (444 B.C. plus A.D. 33), which equals 483 years. This is precisely A.D. 33, the year Jesus died in Jerusalem.

4. See Geisler, *Baker Encyclopedia of Christian Apologetics,* "Prophecy, as Proof of the Bible."

5. Ruth Montgomery, *A Gift of Prophecy* (New York: Morrow, 1965), viii.

6. See Geisler, *Baker Encyclopedia of Christian Apologetics,* "Nostradamus."

7. John Ankerberg, *Cult Watch* (Eugene, Ore.: Harvest House, 1991), 340.

8. Cited in James Randi, *The Mask of Nostradamus* (Amherst, N.Y.: Prometheus, 1993), 31.

9. Cited in Andre Lamont, *Nostradamus Sees All* (Philadelphia: W. Foulsham, 1943), 71.

10. Lamont, *Nostradamus Sees All,* 71.

11. While the Book of Moses teaches that there is only one God, the Book of Abraham affirms that there are many gods. A comparison of the two reveals the former saying, "I, God," or "I, the Lord God," while the latter affirms "the Gods" or "they [the Gods]" (cf. Book of Moses 2:1, 10, 25; 3:8 [an extract of several chapters from Genesis in the Joseph Smith Translation of the Bible] with Book of Abraham 4:3, 10, 25; 5:8). By 1844 Smith came to believe that "God himself, who sits in yonder heavens, is a man like unto one of yourselves, that is the great secret. . . . I am going to tell you how God came to be God. . . . God himself, the Father of us all dwelt on an earth the same as Jesus Christ himself did. . . . You have got to learn how to be Gods yourselves. No man can learn *[sic]* you more than what I have told you"

(cited in John Taylor, ed., *Times and Seasons* [periodical of the Church of Jesus Christ Latter Day Saints], 5:613–14).

12. For a more detailed discussion, see Norman L. Geisler and William E. Nix, *A General Introduction to the Bible*, revised and expanded (Chicago: Moody Press, 1986), part 2.

13. For these and other citations, see Geisler and Nix, *A General Introduction,* chapter 16.

14. See Geisler and Nix, *A General Introduction,* chapter 16.

15. Roger Beckwith, *The Old Testament Canon in the New Testament Church and Its Background in Early Judaism* (Grand Rapids: Eerdmans, 1986), 427.

16. See Geisler and Nix, *A General Introduction,* chapter 15.

17. See Geisler and Nix, *A General Introduction,* chapters 16 and 17.

18. See Geisler and Nix, *A General Introduction,* 431.

19. Some inspired books are referred to by different names but are contained in the sixty-six inspired books that make up the Bible. These include (1) the letter from Elijah contained in 2 Chronicles 21:12–15; (2) the contents of the records of Samuel, Nathan the prophet, and Gad the seer (1 Chronicles 29:29), which parallel that of 1 and 2 Samuel; (3) the "vision of the prophet Isaiah" (2 Chronicles 32:32), which are probably the same as the book of Isaiah; (4) the other accounts of the life of Jesus (Luke 1:1), which may refer to Matthew and Mark (or to some nonexistent but noninspired records); (5) the "letter from Laodicea" (Colossians 4:16), which may have been Ephesians, written at the same time to be circulated; and (6) a letter to the Corinthians (1 Corinthians 5:9), which may refer to 1 Corinthians, a device known as an "epistolary aorist," which stressed the urgency of the message, a device Paul used elsewhere in the same letter (1 Corinthians 9:15). So there is no evidence any inspired apostolic work is missing from the New Testament.

20. See Keith Marston, *Missionary Pal: Reference Guide for Missionaries and Teachers* (Salt Lake City: Publisher's Press, 1976), 26.

21. See N. L. Geisler and Thomas Howe, *When Critics Ask* (Grand Rapids: Baker, 1992), for a response to these and hundreds of other alleged errors in the Bible.

22. For example, The Book of Mormon teaches monogamy (Jacob 2:23–27), but Joseph Smith later taught polygamy ("Doctrine and Covenants," 132:1–4, 37–39).

23. Kitab al-Wasiyah, 77. Cited in Abdiyah Akbar Abdul-Haqq, *Sharing Your Faith with a Muslim* (Minnesota: Bethany Fellowship, 1980), 62. Also see

Al-Maturidi's defense of the orthodox position against the Mutazilites in John Alden Williams, ed., *Islam* (New York: George Braziller, 1962), 182.

24. See M. H. Haykal, *The Life of Muhammad* (Indianapolis, Ind.: American Trust Publications, 1976), 74.

25. See N. L. Geisler, *Answering Islam* (Grand Rapids: Baker, 1993), 162–63.

26. See, e.g., Norman L. Geisler and Ronald Brooks, *When Skeptics Ask* (Grand Rapids: Baker, 1989); Norman L. Geisler and Thomas Howe, *When Critics Ask* (Grand Rapids: Baker, 1999); Norman. L. Geisler and Ron Rhodes, *When Cultists Ask* (Grand Rapids: Baker, 1997); and Norman L. Geisler, *Baker Encyclopedia of Christian Apologetics* (Grand Rapids: Baker, 1999).

Chapter 8.
Tough Questions about Hinduism and Transcendental Meditation

1. For further reading, see Os Guinness, *The Dust of Death: The Sixties Counterculture and How It Changed America Forever,* revised edition (Wheaton, Ill.: Crossway, 1994).

2. Ravi Zacharias, *Cries of the Heart* (Nashville: W Publishing Group, 2002).

3. Francis A. Schaeffer, *Francis A. Schaeffer Trilogy [The God Who Is There; He Is There and He Is Not Silent; Escape from Reason]* (Wheaton, Ill.: Crossway, 1990).

Chapter 9.
Tough Questions about Yoga, Reincarnation, and Buddhism

1. Bharat Thakur, "A Master Responds," *Time* magazine, Asia, 16 July 2001.

2. C. S. Lewis, *Mere Christianity* (SanFrancisco: HarperSanFrancisco, reprint edition, 2001), 38–39.

Chapter 10.
Tough Questions about Black Islam

1. Cited in James Melvin Washington, ed., *A Testament of Hope: The Essential Writings of Martin Luther King Jr.* (New York: Harper & Row, 1986), 54–55.

2. "Holy War: Rev. Fred Price is fighting the church over racism," *Emerge*, 31 January 1999, 44 (available online at www.elibrary.com).

3. James Cone, *God of the Oppressed* (Maryknoll, N.Y.: Orbis Books, 1997), 49–50.

4. In 1889, the self-proclaimed mahdi, or messiah, from India, Mirza Ghulam Ahmad, founded the Ahmadiyya movement. Ahmad did not just limit his teaching to the social consciousness of India or America but emphasized the need for universal Islamic unity and was the first to organize such a program in America.

5. *The Muslim Almanac*, Detroit: Gale Research Group Inc., 1996.

6. Elijah Muhammad, *The History of Jesus' Birth, Death and What It Means to You and Me* (Atlanta: Secretarius Memps Publications, 1993).

7. "We believe that Allah (God) appeared in the Person of Master W. Fard Muhammad, July 1930; the long-awaited 'Messiah' of the Christians and the 'Mahdi' of the Muslims. We believe further and lastly that Allah is God and besides HIM there is no God and He will bring about a universal government of peace wherein we all can live in peace together." This is statement #12 of What Muslims Believe (What Muslims Believe can be found in any *Final Call* magazine, published by Minister Louis Farrakhan and the Nation of Islam [http://finalcall.com]).

8. See, in particular, Adam Edgerly and Carl Ellis, "Emergence of Islam in the African American Community," on the Internet (http://www.answering-islam.org/ReachOut/emergence.html). See also the interview with Carl Ellis, "How Islam Is Winning Black America," on the Internet (http://www.christianitytoday.com/ct/2000/004/27.52.html). Carl Ellis is a distinguished author and founder of Project Joseph, a ministry designed to address the impact Islam is having on today's black church.

9. "The Honorable Elijah Muhammad, I am here to declare, is risen. The Jesus you have been seeking and waiting for His return has been in your midst for 40 years, *but you knew not who he was*. A Holy One was working among us and it is only now, after he is gone, that we realize who He was. . . . When you turn me [Farrakhan] down and refuse this truth, you are turning down the Lord, the Savior, the Messiah, and Deliverer that you seek. This Deliverer is the Honorable Elijah Muhammad" (cited in Thomas A. Landess and

Richard M. Quinn, *Jesse Jackson and the Politics of Race* [Ottawa, Ill.: Jameson Books, 1985], 94).

10. Cited in *Final Call* magazine 19, no. 19.

11. Original excerpt is from the Mischat-al-Masabih; cited in Edward W. Blyden, *Christianity, Islam and the Negro Race* (Baltimore, Md.: Black Classic Press, 1993; first published in 1888).

12. Buell Gallagher, *Color and Conscience* (New York: Harper & Bros., 1946), 191.

13. Daniel Pipes, "In Muslim America: A Presence and a Challenge," *National Review*, 21 February 2000 (go to http://www.danielpipes.org/article/329).

14. Elijah Muhammad, *The Supreme Wisdom: Solution to the So-called Negroes' Problem* (Newport News, Va.: National Newport News and Commentator, 1957), 43.

15. Wendy Murray Zoba, "Are Christians Prepared for Muslims in the Mainstream?" *Christianity Today* (3 April 2000), 40 (on the Internet at http://www.christianitytoday.com/ct/2000/004/1.40.html).

16. Zoba, "Are Christians Prepared for Muslims in the Mainstream?" 40. See also in this issue Carl Ellis, "How Islam Is Winning Black America," 52 (http://www.christianitytoday.com/ct/2000/004/27.52.html).

17. *Muhammad Speaks*, Black Muslim newspaper (6 June 1959).

18. "Jesus Is Killed," in *The History of Jesus' Birth, Death and What It Means to You and Me.*

Scripture Index

SUBJECT INDEX

Is Your Church Ready?

Ravi Zacharias
and Norman Geisler

Apologetics today may be more relevant and vital than ever. Properly understood, Christianity integrates every dimension of our humanity—spiritual, intellectual, emotional, ethical, and social—and the reasons we provide for our faith must be capable of speaking to all these aspects convincingly. *Is Your Church Ready?* helps you to meet the special challenges of this era in history—especially if you hold a leadership position in the church—and to instill well-balanced apologetics in your church at every level, from the pulpit and in your church's ministries, to the world of home, school, and work in which the members of your church live.

Ideal for use with its companion book, *Who Made God?*—a handbook of answers to over 100 tough questions commonly asked about Christianity—this book features contributions from general editor Ravi Zacharias, John Guest, Peter Grant, Judy Salisbury, J. Budziszewski, and Dean Halverson. You'll find thought-provoking insights on:

- The role of pastors in apologetics
- The three tasks of apologetics
- The crucial role of apologetics in a healthy church
- Restoring the place of apologetics so the needs of the world are met
- Evangelism through preaching, music, and worship
- Preparing parents to handle their children's questions
- What college students need to hear from church leaders
- Building friendships with internationals

Chapters conclude with questions for reflection and discussion so the book can be used in group settings. The book also includes a church leader's annotated resource guide to the best books, articles, organizations, and media resources on apologetics. *Is Your Church Ready?* will motivate and equip you to help your church become one that, both in word and lifestyle, presents compelling evidence for the life-changing gospel of Jesus Christ to a twenty-first-century audience.

Hardcover ISBN: 0-310-25061-7

Pick up a copy at your favorite bookstore!

GRAND RAPIDS, MICHIGAN 49530 USA

WWW.ZONDERVAN.COM